To: Stella

From: Beverley

Enjoy your Cooking

XMAS 2000

Privilege

Privilege

Cooking in the Caribbean for men only
(and for women who care)

By Errol W Barrow and
Kendal A Lee

MACMILLAN
CARIBBEAN

First published 1988 by
MACMILLAN EDUCATION LTD
London and Oxford
Companies and representatives throughout the world

ISBN 0-333-46193-2

16 15 14 13 12 11 10 9   8
07 06 05 04 03 02 01 00 99

This book is printed on paper suitable for recycling and
made from fully managed and sustained forest sources.

Printed in Hong Kong

A catalogue record for this book is available from the
British Library.

Table of Contents

Foreword

Back in 1967 there was a Caribbean Heads of Governments' meeting in Port-of-Spain, Trinidad. The West Indian political greats of the day were there: Dr Eric Williams, Michael Manley, Forbes Burnham and Errol Barrow, and the locals in Trinidad were playing their favourite game – 'If you had to pick one man to be Prime Minister of the entire West Indies, who would you pick?' Bypassing their own Prime Minister, the unanimous popular choice was Errol Barrow – and for very human reasons. Errol Barrow had been seen quietly walking down the street in Port-of-Spain doing his own shopping. It was said throughout the length and breadth of the West Indies that Errol Barrow never used his office to surround himself with pomp and prestige; in fact, he would appear on a Sunday morning at the Grantley Adams airport in Barbados driving his own car, no police or bodyguard in sight, to pick up a friend in transit, and drive him home for breakfast. But best of all, it was known throughout the West Indies that Errol Barrow would do the cooking himself.

Errol Barrow, who died in June, 1987 at

Trinidad crab vendor Courtesy Roger Cambridge

the age of 67, stood out amongst Caribbean politicians not only for the power of his intellect, which was formidable, but for the way, in office or out of it, he had never lost contact with, nor lost the respect and almost awed regard of the voters. A distinguished lawyer, known for the incisiveness of his social and economic analyses, and twice holder of the highest political office in his own country, he was never swayed by humbug, flattery or ceremony. Perhaps his love for, and skill at cooking – an activity to which he applied the same combination of concentration and instinct – had something to do with it. There is something about the love for good food and the care and deliberation of its preparation that keeps one close to the essentials of human life. If one could only guarantee that the effect on other politicians would be the same, one could justifiably demand that the ability to cook – and to cook well – be made a pre-qualification for any election to the office of Prime Minister.

About six years ago, Kendal Lee and his wife Ave, whom we had known for many years, invited us to spend a weekend with them in Barbados. Kendal, who died a mere six weeks after his friend Errol Barrow, was one of those extraordinary human beings who never seemed to come to even within hailing distance of the boundaries of his areas of interest. By profession a dentist, practising in Trinidad & Tobago, he plunged into life with an enthusiastic curiosity that led him to such diverse fields as the restoration of antiques, jazz in all its forms, gardening, art, interior design and fishing, to name but a few of his passions. Over the course of an evening with old friends he was quite likely to get into deep discussions on mysticism, philosophy, politics, the occult, and inevitably, one of his deepest loves – cooking, at

which he was a dedicated master. Kendal Lee's involvement with cooking went back a long way, and was pursued with surgical thoroughness and undisguised delight. He spent long hours experimenting with varieties and methods of cooking, lovingly approaching sauces and spices from different angles and points of view. Knowing Kendal's talents, any opportunity to get together with him and a kitchen was an opportunity to be embraced. We therefore accepted their invitation with great anticipation.

The weekend in Barbados was spent at Errol Barrow's home in Oistins. We arrived on Friday evening late, and were offered a bowl of 'Dipper' Barrow's split pea soup. It was made in traditional West Indian style, with salt pork and dumplings and stayed on the back burner of the stove for the entire weekend. Anyone coming in hungry from an early swim, or waking up ravenous from a nap, would wander into the kitchen and help themselves to what was quite simply one of the most stomach and soul satisfying soups I had ever eaten.

The weekend developed into a kind of cook-a-thon with Kendal and 'Dipper' taking over the kitchen. They cooked all day Saturday, refreshing themselves occasionally with a bowl of split pea soup or an iced drink. By ten o'clock Saturday night they had produced a banquet to which friends and neighbours flocked with justifiable expectation. Watching them cook in the kitchen together was to experience an operation at once totally West Indian and admirably professional. The chopping, pounding, tasting, testing, smelling and serving were done with a minimum of confusion and fuss and an under-current of friendly rivalry which never disturbed their easy concentration. The companionable asides of 'Have you

Sunday Buffet in Barbados   Photography by Willie Alleyne

ever tried it with a little ginger?', or, 'If
you steam it for a few seconds first it
brings out the flavour more', were punctu-
ated with the occasional male grunt as the
house filled with the smells of cooking
almost too much for the other occupants
to bear. It was a magnificent meal, the
cooks beaming with nonchalant modesty,
the guests going back for seconds and
thirds of one speciality or another.

Some of the recipes used that night are
among those in this book. Others have
been developed and refined over the years
– each tested on willing family and friends
in the characteristically relaxed and casual
Caribbean settings by these serious and
talented chefs. They reflect the influences

and cultures – the Chinese, Arab, African,
French, English and East Indian – that
blend together to make the West Indies
and its cuisine the unique experiences that
they are.

Take, for example, some of the traditional Caribbean favourites – known to
and beloved by those intimate with the
West Indies. One of these is *Bul Jol*,
an essential part of a long, lazy Sunday
brunch; another *Souse*, a taste for which
guarantees a Caribbean connection. The
recipes for *Crab Back*, *Flying Fish*,
Jamaican Stamp and Go and *Bajan Jug Jug*
will bring an evocative smile of apprecia-
tion to the lips of those familiar with any
of these dishes. Indeed, the book itself is

IX

such a joy to read that even non-cooks will delight in it. Where else, for example, will you find a recipe for cooking bacon that reads: 'Bacon. Place strips of bacon on a rack in a shallow pan. Select heat at 125°F. Place pan in oven. Go to bed'? Where else will you read about that long known but hitherto undiagnosed malady ignored by modern psychiatrists, 'Kitchen stress'? Where else will you be able to read a treatise on 'How to light a fire' or 'Cooking rice in bed'?

Where will you find recipes for such exotic dishes as *Lemon Grass Fish Fillets wrapped in Banana Leaves* or *Red Snapper with Spinach Stuffing* side by side with skilful variations on older themes such as *Beef Tenderloin, Calypso Birds* and *Lime Chicken*?

You don't have to live in the Caribbean to feel the pull of these dishes. The *Bajan Bouillabaisse*, for example, and the *Seafood Gumbo* will create new memories for seafood lovers all over the world to cherish. The insouciant combination of fresh mint and coriander to flavour vegetables knows neither boundary nor climate to delight. And for those looking for a taste sensation to melt the most conservative of eaters, *Braised Pork Hocks in Tangy Tamarind Sauce* cannot be outdone. Gloria Chu's magical guest appearance provides the secrets of such closely guarded mysteries as *Poached Soy Sauce Chicken* and *Braised Red Snapper with Black Bean Sauce*. Using Caribbean ingredients, adapted to Caribbean tastes, they act as an appropriate complement to such recipes as Errol Barrow's for the ubiquitous *Mettagee* which goes under the aliases *Oil Down* and *Run Down* as it turns up in different Caribbean islands.

What a book! It will provide hours of enjoyment for layman and chef alike and hours more enjoyment for those of Caribbean palate and memory who sample dish by dish the work done by Errol Barrow and Kendal Lee.

Diana Mahabir
1987

This cookbook is a recording of the great pleasure derived from the culinary endeavours of two successful men. Its aim is to share this great joy and to help those who have to prepare one of life's great pleasures – good food!!

Kendal and I met Errol through John and Dorothy Watts in the 1960s. The two men, already outstanding in their different fields, soon found out they shared a keen interest in the kitchen. In spite of busy schedules, they managed to get together for over 20 years in different parts of the world to cook. And what memorable and exciting sessions these were. It was indeed a 'Privilege' for me to share with the two authors the happy relationship that produced such excellent dishes. Errol truly loved to cook and would sometimes croon and dance whilst he pursued his greatest hobby. Kendal was already a good cook when I met him. It never bothered me that he was a better cook! He was constantly creating new recipes. His cooking experiences included courses at Cordon Bleu in Paris and Pru Leith's cooking course in London.

The recipes in this book are only a sample portion of the total recipes the two authors cooked. Friends who tasted the dishes encouraged us to write a cook book.

I have been asked, 'What is this book about?' I have answered simply, 'It is about two accomplished men cooking, and having a fantastic, enjoyable time!!'

Ave Lee
1988

Introduction

Errol W. Barrow

Kendal Lee and I discovered our mutual interest in cooking during the course of one of my annual cruises through the Grenadines, about twenty odd years ago.

I had dropped anchor off L'Anse-aux-epines pronounced 'Lansepeenes' by the residents. Having gone ashore to the house of another old friend, Dr John Watts, to have an unrestricted shower, I discovered that John and his wife Dorothy were having guests in to dinner and that Kendal Lee had been persuaded to supervise the cooking of a Chinese repast. I immediately volunteered to relieve Kendal of one of the ten or twelve courses by preparing the sweet and sour pork.

Ave Lee, herself a connoisseur of good, especially Chinese, food, was sceptical, knowing how much her husband liked elbow room in his kitchen, and wondering what a Bajan lawyer-politician could know about Chinese cooking.

The first was no problem at all because I immediately gathered up a coal pot (West Indian habachi), some coals, the pork and utensils, and withdrew to the backyard and proceeded to prepare my assigned portion of the dinner. The meal was a great success. Since that time I have made my pilgrimages to Port-of-Spain, and experimented with various types of energy fuels and appliances in the kitchens of the Lees, and they have both visited me in Barbados where we have continued our tests and experiments.

Somewhere along the line, friends persuaded us that we should write a book. *Privilege* is the result of our labours.

We had certain clearly defined guide lines.

Firstly, the recipes had to be ones that

Boats off Oistins, Barbados

Photography by Willie Alleyne

the average man could prepare without a great deal of travail.

Secondly, we were not interested in producing a duplication of recipes found in standard cook books whether North American, European or otherwise. Our book had to have a lot of Caribbean influence in content and flavour.

Thirdly, although all our recipes cannot claim to be entirely unknown or original, they had to be tested by us, each and every one, and to be the result of our own experiences as to preparation and emphasis.

Caribbean cooking can be exciting without being necessarily expensive. Historically covering a wide spectrum of cultures – European, Chinese, African, Indian, Mexican, Spanish – a simple everyday meal prepared in a Caribbean home can have many roots.

Cooking is also chemistry. We have tried to explain that metamorphisis from garden to table involves subtle chemical changes which the good chef keeps in mind when deciding the duration and intensity of the cooking process. Basically for men like us, *Privilege* is also *For Women Who Care.*
Errol W. Barrow

Most of the fruit, vegetables, fish and meats used in this book can be obtained in many cities in Europe, Canada and the United States.

Ethnic markets have followed migrations of Caribbean, Latin American and Chinese people to the cities of Europe and North America, particularly since the early 1950s. International restaurants are to be found all over. Asian, (Indian, Thai, Vietnamese, Chinese) and West Indian groceries have established themselves firmly in the major cities of the United States, Canada and England because of the increasingly varied ethnic populations. As a result of the proliferation of these ethnic food markets, so-called 'exotic' ingredients have become readily available to many households.
EWB

Introduction

Kendal A. Lee

My first recollection of meeting Errol Barrow, then Prime Minister of Barbados, was in the mid 1960s during an Easter weekend visit to Grenada (the Isle of Spice), where an annual yacht regatta race from Trinidad to Grenada took place. We were introduced by mutual friends, Dr John Watts, a Grenadian dentist, and his wife Dorothy. John at the time was the Chairman of the West Indies Tourist Board, and Deputy Leader of the then Opposition Party in Grenada. Errol had arrived in Grenada by yacht with a group of friends which included 'Sonny' Shridath Ramphal, Commonwealth Secretary General, who is from Guyana.

Even though I have many friends in eminent political positions, my interests are definitely non-political. Grenada's attraction for me was in the natural physical beauty of its terrain and beaches; the easy, unsophisticated friendliness of the people; the enjoyment of the savoury dishes of lambie souse and lobster which were plentiful on the island. John Watts knew that I liked to cook, and it was customary that I prepared sumptuous meals when I visited him in Grenada. It did not take very long for Errol and me to realise that we shared a common interest in cooking, and I welcomed him to join me as co-chef to prepare the unusual and elaborate dinner at John Watt's house.

Errol was more interested in pursuing his culinary skills in the kitchen, or relaxing with his friends, than in participating in official functions. Eric Gairy, then Premier of Grenada, with a natural bent for protocol and grandiloquent style of living in contrast to Errol's seemingly disarming way of being himself, sought on many occasions to provide a police escort during Errol's stay in Grenada. Errol did not care for this protocol. He drove his own car in Barbados, and regularly went to the local market and grocery alone.

It was said, (and later confirmed by him) that Errol Barrow was driving his car to Bridgetown at one time, and he picked up a couple of tourists who appeared to have lost their way, and took them to their destination. He was so informative and friendly to them that they were moved to ask him about himself. On further questioning, they eventually asked if he was related to the Prime Minister. Only then did he disclose that he was one and the same – Prime Minister of Barbados!

In Trinidad, the various ethnic elements of society have brought their influences into their cuisine. This is shown in the different varieties of dishes that are enjoyed: dhalpourri, paratha and assorted curries have their origins from the people of India. Garlic pork comes from the Portuguese; pastelles and arepas have their origins from Spanish speaking peoples; there are also the popular local dishes that are offshoots of French, African, Chinese and Syrian cooking. All these are known in various Trinidad kitchens. The traditional seasoning herbs as thyme, chive (like scallions or spring onions), celery, onion and garlic are now being extended to include interesting herbs such as mint, basil, coriander (Chinese parsley) and the strongly flavoured 'chadon bene' (there are other spellings that are used for this local herb) which is well known to those who cook local dishes. The Chinese soy sauce is now accepted internationally and,

Jean Baptiste Bay, Blanchisseuse, Trinidad
Courtesy the Trinidad and Tobago Tourist Board

eventually, other soy bean products such as the brown bean and black bean will become as well known and widely used as soy sauce.

The present-day Caribbean cuisine can be viewed as reflecting the West Indian society, as it moves from the agrarian to the industralised leanings. The recipes in this book will show some of the subtle influences brought into Caribbean cuisine by those who have come from other lands and made the West Indies their home.

The title of this book – *Privilege – Cooking in the Caribbean for Men Only* – in no way attempts to demonstrate 'men's lib.' or rights in the kitchen, and it is hoped that the book will provoke constructive comments from the fairer sex, as well as appeal to them. This book is intended to reach the growing number of men like Errol Barrow and myself, who have full-time careers or professions, and who love to cook for the sheer joy of doing so; who find it relaxing as well as enjoyable, and a welcome relief and change from the tensions of their work. This should contribute to their sharing of family life (not chores!) and improve the quality of their lives. We hope we have included recipes which show and help those who would like to prepare a tasty meal quickly – perhaps after work, without prior lengthy preparation. Included also are guidelines for the health and diet conscious; tips on cooking, and anecdotes from personal experiences.

It is hoped that others will be able, after reading this book, to share some of the great enjoyment that can be experienced in the preparation required for what is without doubt the most necessary everyday function – eating and enjoying a good meal.

Kendal A. Lee

Acknowledgements

John and Dorothy Watts who brought us together.
Dame Nita Barrow who got me involved in the kitchen on Saturday mornings as a school boy.
Ave Lee who over the years offered suggestions and allowed us to make her kitchens untidy. And then put it all together.

Errol W. Barrow
Barbados, W.I.
March 1987

My wife Ave, who made this book possible.
All those who have helped to make cooking a most enjoyable experience over the years, especially Sue for invaluable help and support.
Gloria and Gérard, experts in the art of cooking, who helped to inspire me. Becky and those who cooked with me; those who shared recipes with me, as well as those who gave encouragement to the writing of this book.

Kendal A. Lee
Trinidad, W.I.
March 1987

Photography by Willie Alleyne
Stylings by Marie Henderson, Eleanor Chandler and Jeanine Leemans.
My thanks also to Mr Harold McGee for his book *On Food and Cooking*, which I found illuminating.

Photographs of Trinidad and Tobago scenes, courtesy of the Trinidad and Tobago Tourist Board and Roger Cambridge.

Front cover: Privilege: Photography by Willie Alleyne. Styling by Marie Henderson
Back cover: Errol W. Barrow and Kendal A. Lee, 1987
Photography by Willie Alleyne

Kitchen Comments

The recipes in this book have been simplified as best as we could – not too many various seasonings that may be difficult to obtain in the West Indies and elsewhere. I would like you to enjoy and 'feel', not only the taste, but also the preparation, of good cooking – *La Cuisine Sensuelle* – Sensuous Cooking.

To assert my point of simplified cooking and seasoning, I shall give an example of a recipe which I read from a cook book written by a well publicised chef. It was a chicken recipe, and the seasoning mix consisted of: 1. garlic powder, 2. onion powder, 3. white pepper, 4. cayenne pepper, 5. black pepper, 6. salt. In addition to this, onions and celery were sautéed before the chicken pieces with all the above ingredients were put in. Then followed rich chicken stock with the following herbs: 1. sage, 2. oregano, 3. thyme, 4. basil, 5. more cayenne pepper, 6. black pepper, 7. white pepper, 8. salt. The inclusion of so many different herbs and seasonings in this dish would make the taste so overpowering, that the taste of the meat would be completely lost. This particular recipe is a good example of the pitfall of overseasoning food with too many different items.

In contrast to this method of using many different seasonings, the recipe for *Lime Chicken* has very little seasoning in it – basically lime juice, salt and a little stock. But taste it. The chicken is deliciously flavoured with the lime sauce.

Coming back to herbs, if you can obtain them fresh, it is much better than using dried herbs. Fresh herbs can be preserved for a time by freezing or drying. For some herbs like chive, parsley and mint, freezing is recommended, for if dried, their flavour and aroma will deteriorate or be lost.

Freezing herbs can be done by various methods. One is to chop each herb, like chives, dill and basil, finely, and pack separately into ice cube trays topped with cold water, then freeze. The ice cubes can then be removed from the tray and stored in plastic polythene bags and labelled. Cubes can be used as required within a reasonable time – up to 6 months.

Herbs such as parsley, mint, celery and tarragon can be liquidised in a blender, separately, with the addition of a little water. These are poured into ice trays and frozen, and then the frozen cubes are removed from the trays and stored in labelled plastic bags.

Preparing a meal
Hygenic preparation of food is essential to maintaining good health. Care should be taken to make your kitchen environment not only aseptic but also aesthetic in appearance. Work counters should be wiped with a clean, damp cloth, and the kitchen floor swept and cleaned with a mild antiseptic in the detergent, and then mopped dry. All kitchen utensils and wares to be used should be thoroughly washed and cleaned and readily available for use. 'Kitchen Stress' should be avoided wherever possible by those who cook regularly.

Several containers or bowls of various sizes should be available for storing chopped seasonings, vegetables and meats. A roll of thin polythene film should be always at hand so that open containers or bowls can be covered and sealed with this film. This requirement of covering every

Hibiscus flowers are found throughout Trinidad and Tobago
Courtesy the Trinidad and Tobago Tourist Board

bowl with polythene avoids possible food contamination by flies and germs or bacteria. The added advantage of using transparent polythene as a covering is that you can easily identify the various seasonings, vegetables and other contents of the bowls. When arranged neatly, the ingredients in the bowls can be pleasing and colourful in appearance – all advantageous to the wellbeing of the cook. Imagine red tomatoes in one bowl, next to one with green peppers, and another with carrots! This is what I mean about kitchen aesthetics; these bowls arranged neatly can be likened to a painting in which the kitchen enthusiast joyfully participates.

Have a large bowl at hand to be used as a collector of discarded trimmings, peelings, etc. This saves time in walking to the garbage bin intermittently to dispose of these items. The bowl can then be emptied when you are finished the food preparation, or when it is filled. It also encourages you to clean up your work areas constantly. I detest a disordered, cluttered up kitchen. When I have finally prepared a recipe to be cooked, or when I have finished cooking, my kitchen is as clean as when I started. A kitchen lover should enjoy every aspect and phase of cooking from food preparation to serving the dish.

Your work areas should be well lighted and ventilated with the kitchen sink readily accessible, and centrally located. A knife sharpener should be a regular item to keep in the kitchen, for sharp knives make the cook's work less stressful and more efficient and quick. The meat or vegetable cutting board should be large enough so as not to make you feel cramped when working.

KAL

Carnival costume depicting fish — Trinidad   Courtesy and Trinidad and Tobago Tourist Board

Fish

Arabic Fish

Red Snapper: 1, about 3 to 4 lbs, whole
Lime juice: ½ cup
White pepper: ¼ teaspoon
Onions: 4, 2 chopped and 2 grated
Olive oil: 2 tablespoons
Parsley: ½ cup, chopped
Garlic: 1 level teaspoon, crushed
Tahini paste: ½ cup
Almonds: ½ cup *and*
pine nuts, fried in butter until brown: ½ cup

Season fish with lime juice, garlic, grated onions, salt and pepper. Bake fish covered with foil for 20 minutes or until cooked. Leave to cool on a dish. Fillet the top side of the fish, exposing the bone along the centre. Set fillet aside. Lift off the backbone and discard.
Sauté 2 chopped onions till tender, and pour over centre of fish, then replace the fillet over the onions on the centre of the fish to its original position, so the fish is re-shaped.
Pour tahini sauce over fish. Sprinkle chopped parsley, fried almonds and pine nuts over fish, and decorate with lime wedges.

Tahini Sauce

Tahini paste: ½ cup
Lemon juice: ½ cup
Garlic: 1 level teaspoon, crushed
White pepper: ¼ teaspoon
Olive oil: 1 tablespoon
Water: ¼ cup
Salt: a pinch

Beat all the ingredients together in a blender to make Tahini Sauce.

Bajan Bouillabaisse

Onions: 2 large, finely chopped
Garlic: 3 cloves, minced
Tomatoes: 3 large, peeled and chopped
Tomato purée: 2 tablespoons
Thyme: 1 tablespoon, finely minced
Parsley: 1 tablespoon, minced
Lime juice: 2 teaspoons
Olive oil: 5 tablespoons
Butter: 2 tablespoons
Flour: 3 tablespoons
Assorted fish fillets Red Snapper, Grouper, Mackerel: 3 lbs, cut into pieces
Shrimps: 1½ lbs, cleaned and de-veined
White wine: 1 cup
Salt: 1 teaspoon
White pepper: 1 teaspoon
Fish stock (see recipe for Seafood Stock): 2 quarts

Heat the olive oil in a large pot and sauté the onions and minced garlic. Add butter and keep heat at low-medium until onions are golden. Stir the flour in for 3 minutes. Add the tomatoes, thyme, parsley, pepper, fish stock, tomato purée and wine. Bring to the boil and simmer for 45 minutes. Add the fish fillet pieces, shrimp and lime juice. Remove from heat and keep pot covered for 15 minutes. Add salt if necessary to correct flavour to your taste. Serve hot.

Baked Fish in Mushroom and Wine Sauce

Fish: 1 large grouper, red or similar,
  3 to 4 lbs
Chive: 1 tablespoon, chopped
Parsley: 1 tablespoon, chopped
Garlic: 1 teaspoon, finely minced
Corn oil: 5 tablespoons
Lime juice: from 1 peeled fresh lime
Rum (Barbados or Trinidad): 1 fluid oz
Salt and black pepper: to taste or $\frac{1}{2}$
  teaspoon each

Bone fish and cut into 2″ cubes. Season with all other ingredients except oil and let marinate for about 1 hour.
Sauté fish in hot oil until crisp. Remove fish from fire and drain off excess oil. Place in baking dish and prepare sauce.

Sauce for Baked Fish

Butter: 2 tablespoons
Flour: 4 tablespoons
Onion: 3 tablespoons, minced
Milk: 2 cups
Wine: 4 tablespoons, white
Mushrooms (canned): 4 oz, sliced
Cheese – Cheddar or similar: $\frac{1}{2}$ cup, diced
Salt and pepper: to taste
Cheese – Parmesan or similar:
  2 tablespoons

Put milk on fire. Blend flour with a little water. Add butter, salt and pepper to milk. Just before milk comes to the boil, add flour mixture and stir well, until mixture thickens. Add onions, wine, mushrooms and cheese until melted and cooked. Pour over fish in baking dish, sprinkle Parmesan cheese on top and bake at 400°F for about 30 minutes.

Fishing with a seine net in the sea off Barbados

Photography by Willie Alleyne

Baked Red Snapper with a Spinach Stuffing

Red Snapper (leave whole): about 4 to
    5 lbs
Pepper: 1 teaspoon cayenne
Garlic: 1 clove, freshly minced
Scallions (chives): 1 tablespoon, chopped
Salt: 1 teaspoon
Fish stock: 1½ cups
Butter: 2 oz, melted
Lime juice: juice of 1 lime
Cornstarch: 1 teaspoon

The fish should be scaled and cleaned thoroughly with the under portion slit to remove the gut.

Dry properly and season with pepper, salt, scallions, garlic and lime juice. Let stand for 45 minutes.

Fill the cavity of the fish with the spinach stuffing.

Place the fish in a baking-serving dish and brush with half of the butter. Pour the fish stock and rest of the butter into the dish. Heat oven to 375°F and bake for 45 minutes, basting whenever necessary.

Remove dish from oven. Use a bulb baster or spoon to remove juices into a saucepan. Thicken sauce over a medium heat with 1 teaspoon cornstarch dissolved in 1 tablespoon water. Pour over fish. Garnish with cut lime wedges and serve.

Spinach Stuffing

Spinach leaves: 1 or 2 bunches, fresh
Chives or spring onions: ½ cup, chopped
Lime juice: juice of 1 lime
Salt: to taste (approximately ½ teaspoon)
Black pepper: 1 teaspoon
White bread crumbs: 1 cup
Milk: 3 tablespoons

Remove hard stems from spinach and cook in boiling water for about 8 minutes until tender. Drain off water and set aside to cool. Squeeze spinach to remove as much water as possible until mass is homogeneous and pulpy.

In a skillet melt the butter and cook the spinach to remove as much moisture as possible. Remove from heat and add the lime juice, bread crumbs, salt, milk and pepper. Blend well.

Season with more lime juice and salt if necessary to correct the flavour.

Glass bottom boat at Buccoo Reef, Tobago Courtesy the Trinidad and Tobago Tourist Board

Braised King Fish with Coo-Coo Balls

King fish: 6 steaks (about 2 lbs)
Maraval herbs (see Glossary): 2
  tablespoons, minced
Hot pepper sauce (see Sauces): 1 teaspoon
Garlic: 2 cloves, crushed
Salt and cayenne pepper: 1 teaspoon each
Tomato ketchup: 2 tablespoons
Lime juice: from 1 peeled lime
White wine: 2 tablespoons
Water: ½ cup
Onions: ½ cup, minced
Corn oil: 3 tablespoons
Cornstarch: for dusting fish

Season fish steaks with herbs, onions, salt, pepper and lime juice.
Marinate for 1 hour. Dust steaks lightly with cornstarch.
Heat oil in skillet, add garlic. When browned, remove. Add steaks to pan-fry for 2 minutes on each side then add wine, ketchup, hot sauce and water. Cover and cook slowly for 8 minutes. Add more salt for correct flavour if necessary.

Cornmeal Coo-Coo

Fresh ochroes (okras): ½ lb
Clear stock: 1½ cups
Salt: ½ teaspoon
Yellow cornmeal (promasa): 5 oz

Cut off the end stalks of the ochroes and section the ochroes in ½″ pieces.
Put ochroes, stock and salt in a pot and bring to a boil. Cover and cook slowly for 12 minutes, when the ochroes should be tender.
Remove the cover and sift the cornmeal slowly into pot, stirring continuously until the mixture becomes doughy, and leaves the bottom and sides of the pot.
In a well-greased round bowl, put a spoonful of the mixture into the bowl, and rotate the bowl so that the dough forms a ball.
Transfer to a dish. Keep adding a spoonful, one at a time, of the mixture in the greased bowl, to shape into balls until all are done.
Braised King fish and coo-coo balls go well together.

Krispy Fish

Red Snapper, Bass or round white fish:
  1, approximately 3 lbs
Lime or lemon: 1
Flour: 1 cup, white
Salt: 1 teaspoon
White pepper: a dash
Cooking oil: 2 pints
Egg: 1
Arrowroot (St Vincent or cornstarch):
  2 tablespoons
Ginger: 1 teaspoon, powdered
Scallion: 2 blades, chopped
Hot peppers: 6 or 8, finger peppers
Sugar: 2 tablespoons, brown
Onions: 2 medium
Baking powder: 2 teaspoons
Vinegar: 1 tablespoon

Remove gut, tail, dorsal fin and scales of fish. Dissolve 2 teaspoons of baking powder in a bowl of water and clean the fish in this solution for 2 to 3 minutes. Rinse and dry. Make 2 diagonal incisions on each side of fish. Cut lime or lemon in half and rub inside and outside. Place in refrigerator for at least 2 hours to dry further.
Beat egg in a bowl and sprinkle with salt and white pepper while beating.
Cover fish inside and out, including the head, with beaten egg. On a flat plate or dish, mix flour, arrowroot and powdered ginger.
Heat oil in deep iron frying pan or 2″ deep electric pan to 370°F until it just begins to smoke. Cover fish with flour mixture and shake off excess. Place in hot oil and turn two or three times until cooked and rich golden brown in colour. In a smaller skillet, burn slightly the onions, scallion and finger peppers in two tablespoons of hot oil from fish pan. Remove from skillet. Throw in sugar and some powdered ginger in same skillet until the sugar is melted. Mix 1 tablespoon of flour mixture in 1 cup cold water and 1 tablespoon vinegar. Throw into the skillet and stir into a thick sauce. Place cooked fish in serving dish. Place burnt peppers, onion and scallion on fish. Pour sauce over all and serve hot.

French Angelfish at Buccoo Reef, Tobago
Courtesy the Trinidad and Tobago Tourist Board

Braised Red Snapper with Black Bean Sauce

Corn oil: 4 tablespoons
Red Snapper (whole): 1 to 1½ lbs
Black beans (Chinese tow-see): 1½
    tablespoons, crushed
Root ginger: 2 slices, finely shredded
Garlic: 1 large clove, crushed
Sherry wine: 1 tablespoon
Sugar: ½ teaspoon
Dark soy: 3 tablespoons
Tomato: 1
Chive, scallions or green onions: 2 stalks
Water: ½ cup
Salt: pinch

Wash black beans by rinsing in water. Add garlic and ginger and crush to a paste. Add sugar, wine and soy sauce. Mix thoroughly. Set aside.
Clean and brown fish in oil on both sides. Lower heat. Add pre-mixed spice sauce to fish. Pour this directly over the fish keeping it on the fish. Now slowly add the water around the fish, being careful not to wash spice off the fish.
Cover and simmer until fish eye pops up (about 5 to 7 minutes at slow boiling point), basting with the liquid in the pan a couple of times. Remove the fish to a platter. Garnish with sliced tomato and diced green onions placed decoratively on top of the fish. Add remaining sauce to cover the fish completely. Serve hot.

Carite Cutlets in Coconut Milk

Carite (Mackerel) fillets: 1 lb, cut in
    3″ pieces
Garlic: 1 clove, minced
Salt and white pepper: to taste
Fresh lime juice: 2 tablespoons
Thyme: 1 sprig, minced
Parsley: 1 tablespoon, minced
Coconut milk (see recipe): 1 cup
Butter: 2 tablespoons
Cornstarch (St Vincent arrowroot):
    1 teaspoon
Corn oil: for deep frying

Season fish with garlic, 1 tablespoon lime juice, salt and white pepper and thyme. Marinate for one hour. Dredge fish pieces in flour and deep fry for 2 minutes in corn oil. Drain and set aside. Sauté onions in heated butter until glazed. Add coconut milk, parsley and 1 tablespoon lime juice; add salt if desired. Return fish pieces to pan, cover and cook on low heat for 10 minutes. Thicken gravy with 1 teaspoon cornstarch dissolved in 1 tablespoon of water. Serve hot.

Escovitch Fish

Fish – Ning Nings, Jacks: about 6, small
Herrings or Snapper: (up to 10″ long)
Lime juice: from 2 peeled limes
Salt and black pepper: to taste, or $\frac{1}{2}$
  teaspoon
Deep fat: to fry fish
Onions: 2 medium
Hot peppers: 3
Christophene (chayote): 1, cut into long,
  thin strips
Vinegar: 1 cup
Pimento grains (whole allspice):
  1 teaspoon
Cooking oil (vegetable or corn):
  2 tablespoons
Flour or breadcrumbs: to fry fish

1. Clean and scale, leave on head, and leave bone in fish.
2. Rub with juice of 2 limes. Mix some salt and black pepper together and rub, particularly on inside.
3. Fry fish in deep fat without dredging in flour or breadcrumbs.
4. Drain on brown paper or paper towel, then place fish on a platter side by side.
5. Take 2 fair sized onions, and 3 hot peppers and cut in rings about $\frac{1}{8}$″ deep. Also cut 1 christophene into long strips, thin.
6. To paragraph 5, add 1 cup vinegar, a teaspoon of pimento grains, salt and black pepper to taste, or $\frac{1}{4}$ teaspoon each, 2 tablespoons cooking oil, preferably vegetable or corn oil.
7. Place all ingredients in paragraphs 5 and 6 in a pan and simmer for 10 minutes. Remove from stove and pour over fish and serve.

Glutinous Fish Mixture

Fish: Use King fish, Carite – 4 lbs
Garlic: 2 teaspoons, minced
Chive: 4 tablespoons, chopped
Lime: juice of 1
Sesame oil: $\frac{1}{2}$ teaspoon
Vinegar: 1 teaspoon
Cornstarch: 1 teaspoon
Salt: to taste

Fillet the fish and use a spoon to scrape away the flesh. Set aside. Dip your fingers in a bowl of salt water and knead the fish mass until it is pulpy and well blended. Take the fish mass, as much as you can hold in one hand, and throw it against a meat board. Pick it up several times, dipping your fingers into the salt water from time to time, until it is very sticky and glutinous. This preparation should take about 6 to 8 minutes.

Glutinous Fish Balls

Glutinous fish mixture:
  see recipe for ingredients

Place the glutinous fish mixture in a bowl and introduce the seasoning ingredients and blend well, adding salt if necessary. Shape the mixture into balls 1″ in diameter or flatten into steaklike shapes 2″ × 4″ size. In these shapes, the fish balls or steaks can then be fried or boiled in soup. This is a unique method of preparing fish into a glutinous, firm substance which, when cooked, has a firm, meaty consistency. It can also be used as a stuffing. When cooked, it can be sliced and sautéed with vegetables or put into soups. Many interesting recipes can develop from this method. Carite or king fish are most suitable for this preparation.

Glutinous Fish Slices with Green Beans

Glutinous fish mixture: 1 portion
  (see recipe)
Green beans: 2 cups
Soy sauce (light): 1 tablespoon
Sugar: 1 teaspoon
Root ginger, fresh: 2 'thumbs', shredded
White pepper: a dash
Chive or scallions: 1 tablespoon, chopped
Corn oil: 2 tablespoons
Sesame oil: a few drops

Scald green beans in boiling water for 1 minute and drain.
Form fish mixture into steaks 2″ × 4″. Cook 'steaks' in pot of boiling water for 2 minutes. Drain and set aside to cool. Cut cooked fish steaks into 2″ × $\frac{1}{4}$″ slices. Heat oil in a frying pan and sauté fish slices together with chive, ginger and white pepper for 1 minute. Add beans with sugar, soy sauce and sesame oil. Cover for 2 to 3 minutes.
Serve immediately – hot.

Lemon Grass Fish Fillets Wrapped in Banana Leaves

Fish fillets: 2$\frac{1}{2}$ lbs Mackerel (Carite or King fish), cut into pieces 3″ × 1$\frac{1}{2}$″
Salt: 2 teaspoons
Onions: 3 medium
Garlic: 4 cloves, minced
Fresh root ginger: 2″ piece, peeled and pounded
Chilli: 1 teaspoon, powder
Cornstarch (St Vincent arrowroot): 2 tablespoons
Lemon grass coconut milk: 1$\frac{1}{3}$ cups
Corn oil: 4 teaspoons
Cabbage or patchoi leaves: 20 cut in half
Banana leaves: 20 approximately 7″ × 7″

Put the fish pieces in a bowl and rub lightly with half the salt. Set aside. Thinly slice $\frac{1}{2}$ onion, then pound or purée the remaining onions. Mix the puréed onions to a paste with the remaining salt, garlic, ginger, chilli powder and cornstarch. Add the lemon flavoured coconut milk to the onion paste with the oil and sliced onion. Mix well.
On each banana leaf, place 1 piece of cabbage, then top with a little of the paste mixture. Lay on a piece of fish, add a little more paste mixture on the fish, then cover with another piece of cabbage or patchoi. Fold the banana leaf to enclose the filling, with the edges tucked under to seal it. Steam the parcels for 20 minutes. The wrappings can be removed before serving hot, or the parcels can be served on the table, and the wrappings removed just before eating.

Poached Fish Gloria   Photography by Willie Alleyne. Styling by Eleanor Chandler

Lemon Grass Coconut Milk

Lemon or fever grass: 1 stalk
Dried coconut: 1 cup, grated

Lemon grass grows easily in the West Indies. It is popularly known as fever grass. The blades are cut and steeped in boiling water as a herbal remedy for reducing fever, and therefore the name 'fever grass' is more commonly used, although it imparts a lemon flavour. It is also a good *digestif* for upset stomachs when the blades of the grass are drawn like tea – boiling water is poured on the grass and the hot lemon grass tea is used.
Put 1 stalk with the attached blades of lemon grass tied into a knot in a pan of 3 cups boiling water and simmer for 15 minutes. Remove lemon grass from water. Put grated coconut in boiling water (about 2 cups), remove from stove. After 10 minutes strain off the coconut 'milk' and reserve $1\frac{1}{3}$ cups.

Poached Fish Gloria

Red Snapper fish: 1, whole $1\frac{1}{2}$ to 2 lbs
Corn oil: 3 tablespoons
Sesame oil: 2 teaspoons
Soy sauce (light): 2 tablespoons
Chive or scallions: 2 stalks, thinly sliced 1″ lengths
Fresh root ginger: 4 slices, shredded in thin strips

Put on a large pot of water to boil. When water is boiling, immerse the fish in water, reduce heat to a simmering level, and cook for 10 to 15 minutes.
Remove fish, and place on serving dish, draining off excess water. Lay sliced chive and shredded ginger spread out on top of the fish. Heat corn oil and sesame oil in a pan until the oil starts to smoke. Pour oil slowly on the fish, followed by the light soy.
Spoon the sauce over the fish several times, and serve hot.

Red Fish Fiesta

Red fish (Snapper): 1 whole, about 3 lbs
Tomatoes: 2 medium, chopped
Tomato sauce (see recipe): 2 tablespoons
Sweet peppers: 2 medium, chopped
Salt and black pepper: to taste or 1
  teaspoon
Butter: 2 tablespoons
Onion: 1 medium, chopped
Garlic: 1 clove, minced
Lime juice: from 1 peeled lime
Cornstarch (St Vincent arrowroot):
  1 teaspoon
Corn oil: 2 tablespoons
Grated Cheddar cheese: 2 tablespoons

Scale and clean fish thoroughly, taking out insides. Lay fish flat on a board and, using a sharp knife, cut away one side of the fish from below the head to above the tail. You will now have a fillet of fish. Set aside the main part of the fish. Cut up the fillet into 1″ pieces. Remove and discard the centre backbone of the fish. Lay the rest of the fish on a baking dish. Season fish pieces with cornstarch, garlic, black pepper and salt. Heat butter in a frying pan and quickly sauté the onions and fish pieces.
Remove into a bowl and add sweet peppers, tomatoes, lime juice and tomato sauce. Shape mixture over the fish. Sprinkle with grated cheese and bake at 375°F for 20 minutes. Remove from oven and serve.

Red Fish Fiesta

Photography by Willie Alleyne. Styling by Marie Henderson

Red Snapper Maraval

Red Snapper: 1 whole fish about 4 lbs
Garlic: 1½ cloves, finely minced
Salt: 1 teaspoon, or to taste
Pepper (white): to taste
Rum – Trinidad or Barbados: 1 fluid oz
Maraval herbs: chive, thyme, celery,
    parsley – 1 bunch minced
Large pan to hold fish

Season the fish with the garlic, salt, pepper, rum and half of the minced herbs, and marinate for 1 hour.

Sauce for Red Snapper Maraval

Onions: 1¼ cups minced
Butter: 3 tablespoons
Wine: 1 cup white
Sugar: 2 teaspoons
Lime juice: from 1 peeled lime
Cornstarch: 1 teaspoon
Salt: to taste
Flour: 2 tablespoons

Drain the seasoned fish, dust in flour and fry for 8 to 10 minutes in hot oil until skin is crisp. Remove and drain fish by placing on paper towels.

Sauté the other half of the herbs and onions in butter for 8 to 10 minutes on a low heat until onions are tender and transparent. Then add wine, sugar, salt and ½ cup water. Place fish in the pan with the sauce, cover and cook on low flame for 10 minutes. Gently turn the fish on to the other side, cover and cook again for another 10 minutes. Remove fish and place on serving dish. Sauce will then be left in the pan. Thicken this sauce with cornstarch dissolved in about 1 tablespoon of water. Pour thickened sauce over fish and serve hot.

Flying Fish

Found and caught in the waters off Barbados and Tobago, flying fish are bought in the fish markets whole, but should be gutted and filleted before you take them home.

Filleted flying fish may be obtained in supermarkets in frozen packages. Allow to thaw to room temperature before cooking. Season the fillets with local herbs such as thyme, chive and oregano. Add salt and pepper to taste.

Beat an egg in a bowl. Dip the fish in this. Dredge in a plate of flour or mixture of flour and breadcrumbs. Fry in iron skillet until golden brown. Do not overcook.

Flying fish may also be rolled after being seasoned and steamed. Squeeze the juice of a fresh lime over the fillets and serve hot on a platter.

Smoke-Flavoured Fish Slices　　　　　Photography by Willie Alleyne. Styling by Eleanor Chandler

Stamp and Go (Jamaica)

Fish cakes of a kind elsewhere

Flour: 1 cup
Saltfish: 1 cup, soaked for 2 hrs then shredded
Onion: 1, finely chopped
Green seasoning (chive): 2 oz, finely chopped
Hot pepper: $\frac{1}{2}$ red, finely chopped
Baking powder: 1 teaspoon
Cooking oil: 1 cup

Gradually add about $\frac{1}{2}$ cup cold water to flour and make into a smooth batter. Add all the other ingredients and stir with a wooden spoon. Heat oil in small iron skillet and drop in mixture – $\frac{1}{2}$ tablespoon at a time. Turn when lightly browned. Remove and drain on a flat dish with paper towel.

Smoke-Flavoured Fish Slices

Fish fillets: 1 lb (white fish or similar)
Ginger root: 8 slices, finely shredded
Soy sauce: 10 tablespoons
Dry white wine: 2 tablespoons
Five-season spice powder: 2 teaspoons
Sugar: 8 tablespoons
Corn oil: for deep frying
Boiling water: $2\frac{1}{2}$ cups

Marinate fish for at least 4 hours in ginger, soy sauce and wine. Drain and save liquid for use later. Deep fry in oil until crisp, then marinate in a syrup made with $2\frac{1}{2}$ cups boiling water, 2 teaspoons five-season spice powder, and 8 tablespoons sugar, for a few minutes. Drain and serve hot or at room temperature.

13

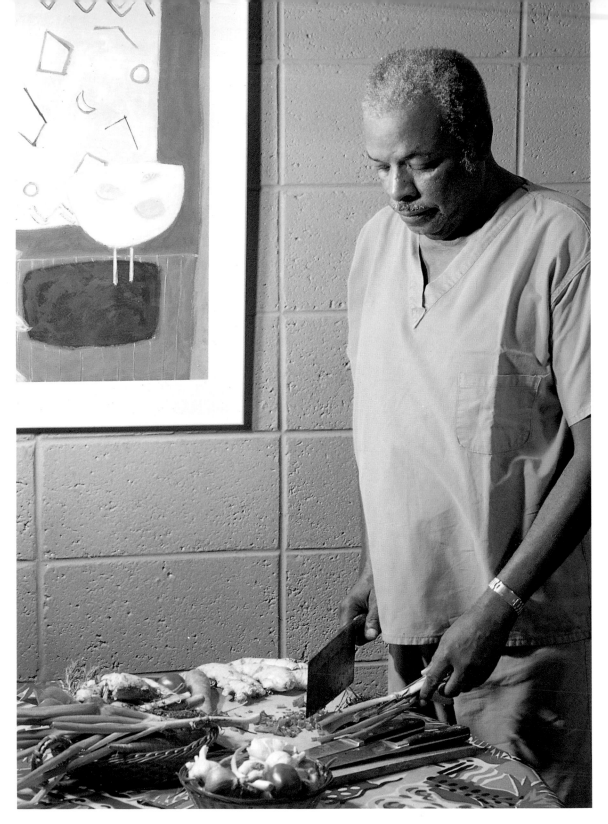

Errol Barrow in the kitchen

Photography by Willie Alleyne

14

Kitchen Stress

Kitchen stress is that elusive ingredient that keeps cropping up most times when you have set out to prepare a grand meal for your dinner guests. Your enthusiasm, however, quickly wanes in proportion to stress situations encountered during the meal preparation, and reaches a point where the effort becomes a chore. Eventually, the meal is prepared, and you sigh with welcome relief amid the untidiness of unwashed dishes and pots, discarded trimmings of vegetables and soiled counters. Then you casually look at your watch and suddenly realise that you have less than half an hour in which to get dressed and receive your guests!

This description may be taken to the extreme, but it happens to us at one time or another in varying degrees. Subsequent examples will demonstrate to you how kitchen stress can dampen your enjoyment of cooking. How often do you find that the pot or pan you want is located on the shelf of a lower cupboard with several pots stacked above it? Then, having made the uncomfortable effort to bend down and stoop to remove and replace the pots in order to retrieve the one you want, you discover that the pot cover is not in the same place. Eventually, it is found in another cupboard. This is what I call 'Kitchen stress'.

The dish or bowl you are looking for is on the top shelf on the overhead cupboard. You have to stretch and reach to remove the front row of plates before you can get at your dish. Yes! It is the bottom dish above which others are stacked. What about the kitchen knives or meat cleaver?

They have been misplaced or cunningly hidden in a drawer overcrowded with too many items. Then you go to slice or cut your meat and vegetables neatly, but the knife has become dull from being used or abused for purposes for which it was never intended. Believe it or not, some member of the household may have used your sharp kitchen knife when doing carpentry! You look for the stone to sharpen the blade, but you can't remember if it is kept in the kitchen or the store room.

The neatly covered metal containers, all uniform in appearance and size, look attractive in the far corner of the kitchen counter. But you can't remember which one contains the flour or the sugar, for they all look alike, and are not marked. It usually happens to be the last container you uncover that stores the ingredient you want.

The refrigerator may look spick and span on the outside, but open the door, and you are confronted, more often than not, by a disarray of various plastic boxes or bowls of left overs, sauces, etc, and the small pyrex bowl of ingredients that you are looking for is completely hidden.

In the freezer, the parcel of shrimps is unidentifiable, and can only be retrieved after removing similar frozen parcels from above and in front of the one you want.

These are some of the many examples of kitchen stress situations we encounter during the use of the kitchen. Then there are indirect stresses, unwittingly imposed by the traditional concept of kitchen layouts.

Many kitchens are designed by architects or designers, who know little about cooking, and consequently are oblivious, even insensitive, to the kitchen user's requirements for an efficient and functional kitchen. The traditional kitchen may look beautiful with the neatly arranged drawers and cupboards and work counters. But what about the items and utensils inside the drawers and cupboards? How do we retrieve them easily, and without undue strain? The designer is not usually concerned about this function. That is your problem. He may want to hide all these items inside the closed drawers and cupboards and render a beautiful elevation to the home owner or prospective purchaser. *KAL*

Oleander blooms on the beach at Prospect, St James, Barbados   Photography by Willie Alleyne

Shell Seafood

Shell Seafood

You will find that the longer you cook shell seafood (shrimp, lobster, lambie, etc), the tougher they get. In cooking shrimp, it is better not to place them on a fire at all, unless you are deep frying in batter. Boil water and pour over shrimp and remove as soon as you get the texture you require – usually as soon as they lose their transparency.

Lobster should be live when you buy them. To kill them they should be plunged into a large kettle of boiling water – the largest you have. Remove the lobster from the water with tongs just as soon as the colour changes to pink. Remove tail from body by circling with sharp pointed knife. Press tail on table with a small cutting board, to break the shell, which will crack along the middle of the back. Slit back and remove the alimentary canal. The legs and claws can be broken by hand, or with assistance of a nutcracker, and the meat removed.

Small lobsters may be bisected from top to bottom. They should be washed and served in the shell.

EWB

Sea Food Gumbo

Ochroes: 8$\frac{1}{2}$ cups, cut up
White pepper: 1$\frac{1}{2}$ teaspoons
Onions: 2 cups, finely cut
Tomatoes: 2 cups, peeled and chopped
Garlic: 2 cloves, minced
Fresh thyme: 2 teaspoons, minced
Celery: 1 cup, chopped
Sweet pepper: 1 cup, chopped
Basic seafood stock (see recipe): 10 cups
Butter: $\frac{1}{4}$ lb
Shrimp: 1 lb medium
Blue crab: 1 cleaned and sectioned
Fish slices: $\frac{1}{2}$ lb (red snapper fillet)
Vegetable oil: 3 tablespoons

Heat oil in pot. Add 6 cups of ochroes. Cook for 3 minutes. Add white pepper. Continue cooking until well browned, scraping bottom of pot with spoon to blend. Stir in the onions and garlic and cook for another 5 minutes. Add 1 cup of stock and cook for 5 minutes. Stir in tomatoes and cook for another 5 minutes. Add 2 more cups of stock. Put in the chopped celery, thyme and sweet peppers and cook for about 30 minutes. Add the butter and remaining 7 cups of stock, stirring well. Bring to a boil and simmer for 45 minutes. Add the remaining 2$\frac{1}{2}$ cups of ochroes and simmer for 10 minutes. Then add the shrimp, crab meat and fish slices. Bring to a boil and remove from heat. Add fresh lime juice and season gumbo with salt to taste.

To serve, place a mounded $\frac{1}{4}$ cup of rice in the centre of each serving bowl. Spoon 1$\frac{1}{2}$ cups of gumbo around the rice. Sprinkle with chopped chives.

Fried Prawn Slices with Sour Sauce

Prawns: 8 (about 1¼ lbs)
Egg white: 2 tablespoons
Salt: ½ teaspoon
Cornstarch (St Vincent arrowroot):
  1 tablespoon and ⅓ cup for coating fish
Garlic slices: 2 teaspoons
Mushrooms: 2 tablespoons
Green peas: 2 tablespoons
Carrot: 2 tablespoons, scalded and sliced
Corn oil: 6 cups

Sour Sauce

Sugar: 3 tablespoons
Vinegar: 3 tablespoons, brown
Stock: 6 tablespoons
Salt: ½ teaspoon
Cornstarch (St Vincent arrowroot): 2
  tablespoons
Sesame oil: ¼ teaspoon

De-vein prawns, split lengthwise leaving ends of tail shells attached to prawns. Flatten, pat and dry. Split crosswise into 2 pieces (1 with tail end, the other without). Place in bowl and mix with egg white, salt and 1 tablespoon cornstarch. Marinate for about ½ hour. Coat each piece with cornstarch lightly.

Heat oil in pan. Deep fry prawns for about 30 seconds until cooked. Remove prawns and drain off oil from pan.

Reheat 3 tablespoons of oil in the same pan. Stir fry the garlic for a few seconds, then add the mushrooms, carrots and green peas. Stir a few seconds again. Mix and pour ingredients in the sour sauce and bring to a boil. Turn off the heat and put the fried prawns into the sauce. Sprinkle in 1 teaspoon of hot oil. Mix well. Remove to a platter and serve hot.

Jacketed Shrimp in a Spicy Sauce

Shrimp: 12 large, in shell
Garlic: 1 clove, chopped
Root ginger: 4 slices, chopped
Chive or scallions: 2 tablespoons
Corn oil: 4 tablespoons
Hot or chilli sauce: ½ teaspoon
Tomato ketchup: 4 tablespoons
Worcester sauce: 1 tablespoon
Tomato paste: 1 teaspoon
Sugar: 2 teaspoons
Cornstarch (St Vincent arrowroot):
  1 teaspoon
Water: 1 tablespoon
Salt and black pepper: to taste

Make a small slit in the back of each shrimp, and de-vein, leaving the jacket on. In a skillet, sauté shrimps in hot oil for 2 minutes, adding salt and black pepper. Remove shrimp from pan, and place on a dish. Drain off excess oil and reheat pan. Add garlic, chive and ginger, and stir-fry for a few seconds; then add the rest of the sauce ingredients, blending well for 2 minutes. Thicken sauce with cornstarch dissolved in water, and return shrimps to sauce. Cook for another minute or so, and serve hot.

Butterfly Shrimp with Mixed Vegetables

Shrimp: 1 lb, large size
Egg white: 1
Sherry: 1 tablespoon, pale, dry
Garlic: 1 clove, finely minced
Cornstarch (St Vincent arrowroot):
  1 tablespoon
Salt and black pepper: to taste
Baking soda: to clean shrimp

Clean and remove shell from shrimp and de-vein. Slice back of shrimps halfway along the length, and then press flat to a butterfly shape. Do not slice the shrimps completely into two halves.

Blend 2 teaspoons of baking soda well into shrimp. After 2 to 3 minutes, wash shrimp thoroughly to remove all the baking soda, drain in a colander, then dry with paper towels. The shrimp should now have a clean, transparent, glazed appearance. Mix together the sherry, egg white, garlic, salt, pepper and 1 tablespoon cornstarch in a bowl. Add shrimp to mixture and then stir fry in hot oil for 2 to 3 minutes. Transfer to a plate.

Mixed Vegetables

Sweet pepper: 1
Carrot: 1 medium
Chive: 1 tablespoon, chopped
Cauliflower: $\frac{1}{2}$ medium
Soy sauce: 2 teaspoons, light
Sugar: 1 teaspoon
Vinegar: 1 teaspoon, red wine
Stock: 1 tablespoon pork stock or water
Oil: 2 tablespoons
Garlic: $\frac{1}{2}$ teaspoon, minced
Sesame oil: a few drops

Slice vegetables into $1\frac{1}{2}''$ strips. Scald in boiling water for $\frac{1}{2}$ minute. Heat oil in pan, sauté garlic, chive and vegetables for 1 minute. Return shrimp to pan and add sugar, soy sauce, vinegar and stock. Correct flavour with more soy if necessary. Stir fry for 30 seconds. Serve on dish, sprinkling with sesame oil.

Guanapo Gorge, Trinidad   Courtesy Roger Cambridge

Shrimp Baked in a Tangy Wine Sauce

Shrimp: 1¼ lbs large, shelled and de-veined
Chive: 2 tablespoons, chopped
Onions: 2 tablespoons, minced
Milk: 1 cup
Wine: 1 cup, white
Water: ½ cup
Cheese: 2 oz, grated (cheddar or similar)
Garlic: 2 teaspoons, minced
Vinegar: 2 teaspoons, white
Sugar: 2 teaspoons
Butter: 2 oz, melted
Flour: 1 tablespoon
Oil (corn or similar): 5 tablespoons
Salt and pepper: to taste
Parmesan cheese: 1 tablespoon

Season shrimp in garlic, salt and pepper. Add oil to pan on high heat. Add shrimp and stir fry for 2 minutes. Transfer and drain on paper towels on dish.
In another pan, heat butter at low temperature. Add chive, onions and cook for 30 seconds. Add flour and blend into butter. Then pour on the milk, wine and water stirring continuously to blend mixture well. Add cheese (grated), salt and pepper to taste, vinegar and sugar. When mixture is smooth and velvety, add more water if necessary to get this consistency, then return the shrimps to the pan and blend with mixture.
Pour mixture into a baking dish. Sprinkle with parmesan cheese (grated) and bake at 400°F for 10 minutes. Serve hot.

Shrimp in an Egg White Sauce

Shrimp: 12 large, (headless and de-veined)
Chive: 1 tablespoon, chopped
Egg whites: whites of 2 eggs
Stock: ½ cup, rich clear
Cornstarch: 1 teaspoon

To freshen up and clean the shrimp further, you can put them in a bowl of water in which a teaspoon of baking powder is dissolved. Rub the shrimp in the water with your fingers. After a few minutes the water will become cloudy and pinkish. This is the thin film that forms on the surface of the shrimp which needs to be dissolved in order to clean the shrimp thoroughly of any stale odour or taste. Remove and wash the shrimp in clean water. Set aside and drain. The shrimp will have a clean, glazed, translucent appearance after this treatment.
In a pot of boiling stock, cook the shrimp for 2½ to 3 minutes. Remove and place on a serving dish. Mix the cornstarch in a ½ cup of rich stock. Heat to boiling for 2 minutes. Mix in the egg white. Remove from heat stirring sauce constantly. Pour contents over shrimp and sprinkle with chopped chive. Serve hot.

Shrimp Omelette

Shrimp: ½ lb, medium size, shelled and
  deveined
Cabbage and carrot: 1 cup, shredded in
  strips
Bean sprouts: 1 cup
Garlic: 1 teaspoon, minced
Sesame oil: 1 teaspoon
Chive or scallions: 2 tablespoons, chopped
Sugar: 1 teaspoon
Sherry: 1 tablespoon
Oil (corn or similar): 3 tablespoons
Eggs: 6
Cornstarch: 3 teaspoons
Salt and pepper: to taste

Cut shrimps into smaller pieces, season
with garlic, salt, pepper and sherry. Heat
oil in pan, stir-fry shrimp for 1 minute.
Transfer to plate. Scald carrot and cabbage
in boiling water for 30 seconds. Drain and
put in large bowl. Add eggs, cornstarch,
sugar, chopped chive and sesame oil, then
shrimp, to bowl, and mix thoroughly.
Heat frying pan or skillet at low temperature with the addition of just enough oil to
cover the bottom of the pan.
When oil is medium hot, pour a kitchen
spoonful of the mixture into the pan. It
should be slightly brown when cooked.
Turn over and cook the other side. Remove to a plate. Repeat with another
spoonful of the mixture until all are
cooked. They should be of pancake size.

Sauce for Shrimp Omelette

Stock (see recipe): 1 cup chicken or pork
Soy sauce – light: 1 teaspoon
Sherry: 1 teaspoon
Cornstarch: 1 teaspoon

Blend these ingredients and heat in a separate pot to make sauce to pour over the
omelettes. Serve hot.

Stuffed Shrimp

Shrimps: 12 large and 15 small
Chive or scallions: 1 tablespoon, chopped
Garlic: 1 clove, finely minced
Sesame oil: 1 teaspoon
Fat: 4 thin slices pork fat or 2 strips bacon
Sugar: 1 teaspoon
Soy sauce: 2 teaspoons, light
Cornstarch: 1 teaspoon

Clean shrimp and wash thoroughly. Put
aside large shrimps and mince the small
shrimps with the pork fat or bacon and
other ingredients, blending into a fine mixture.
Slice the under portion or 'belly' of each
large shrimp so that it can open out. Insert
your thumb into the cut underportion of
the shrimp while holding it. Flatten out the
shrimp by severing the muscles. This will
prevent the shrimp from curling when it is
being fried. Stuff the minced mixture into
the slits of the large shrimps. Deep fry the
stuffed shrimps in hot oil for about 2
minutes, drain on paper towels and serve –
it is best hot.

Stuffed Shrimp

Photography by Willie Alleyne. Styling by Marie Henderson

Broiled Lobster with Buttered Basil Sauce

The Caribbean 'lobsters' do not have claws, and are really large crayfish – also known as rock lobster. However, they can be just as succulent and delicious in flavour.

There are 3 types of basil which I grow in my herbal garden – the regular, green-leafed type, the purplish or opal basil, which is stronger in aroma, and the finer leafed type, Greek basil, which grows in the Caribbean. This last variety has a slight anise aroma in addition to its basilic flavour. Any variety of basil can be used in this recipe. Basil is a herb much used in Italian recipes, and it imparts an interesting flavour to broiled lobster.

Lobster tails: 4, from 1 to 2 lbs lobsters
Garlic: 2 cloves, minced
Shallots: 2 tablespoons, minced
Basil leaves, fresh: 2 tablespoons, minced
Chive or scallions: 1 tablespoon, chopped
Butter: $\frac{1}{4}$ lb
Corn oil: 1 tablespoon
Salt: $\frac{1}{2}$ teaspoon
Lime: 1 large, cut in wedges

Cut the lobster tails along the length into two halves and place them on a broiler pan. Heat the oil gently with a quarter of the stick of butter and gently fry the shallots and garlic until transparent. Mix in the salt. Spoon the contents in equal amounts on to the 'meat' of the lobster tails. Broil in oven for 10 to 12 minutes.

Melt the remainder of the butter in a heated saucepan and mix in basil and chopped chive.

Serve lobsters (hot) with the buttered basil sauce.

KAL

Lobster Kampala

Kampala is the name of a beach cottage on the West Coast of Barbados. Some years ago, I was staying there when Errol phoned to say that he was coming over for lunch.

I looked in the refrigerator and saw two lobster tails and assorted vegetable ends. Since two tails could not be portioned out for three persons, I decided to do what I could to make a nice meal. I used everything that was on hand, and Lobster Kampala was created.

Lobster tails: 2, cut into $1\frac{1}{2}''$ pieces
Carrot: 1 medium, scraped and cut into thin slices $1\frac{1}{2}''$ long
Pimento pepper: 1, sliced
Cauliflower: 1, cut into flowerets
Fresh ginger root: 2 slices, shredded thinly
Garlic: 1 clove, crushed
Chive or scallion: 2 stalks, chopped
Light soy sauce: 2 tablespoons

Lobster Kampala　　　　　　　　　Photography by Willie Alleyne. Styling by Jeanine Leemans

Sugar: 1 teaspoon
Cornstarch (St Vincent arrowroot):
　1 teaspoon
Light sherry: 1 tablespoon
Stock (chicken or pork): 1 tablespoon
Corn oil: 4 tablespoons

Heat oil in frying pan until very hot. Add garlic, and when it is burned, remove and discard. Sauté chive and ginger for 30 seconds. Add lobster pieces and stir-fry for 2 minutes. Meanwhile, scald the vegetables in boiling water for 2 minutes. Remove and strain. Stir in vegetables.

Mix soy sauce, sherry, sugar, stock and cornstarch. Pour sauce into frying pan, and cook for 2 minutes. Put on serving dish and serve hot.

Martinique Lambie Stew

Fresh lambie: 6, cut in 1″ pieces or 36 small conchs
Lime juice: from 2 peeled limes
Salt and pepper: to taste
Tomatoes: 2 large, or 4 small, chopped
Onions: 1 large, or 2 small, chopped
Thyme: 1 sprig, minced or 1 teaspoon, dried
Butter: 2 tablespoons
Garlic: 4 cloves, crushed
Olive oil: 2 tablespoons

Season lambie with half of the lime juice, chives, salt and pepper to taste. Set aside for 1 hour. Melt butter in heated pan, and add onions and cook until glazed. Then add rest of lime juice, thyme, tomatoes and $\frac{1}{2}$ cup water, and let mixture cook over low heat for 10 minutes. Meanwhile, crush and grind the garlic in a mortar and pestle, or purée with oil, salt and pepper in a blender into a paste. Add lambie to simmering sauce and small amounts of garlic paste, a teaspoonful at a time, during the cooking period until the paste is used up. Simmer on low heat for 45 to 60 minutes.
RB

Martinique Lambie Stew   Photography by Willie Alleyne. Styling by Marie Henderson

Caribbean Shrimp Mould

Shrimps (medium or large): 2 lbs, headless
Onions: 3 small, chopped
Sweet peppers: 2 red and green
Salt: to taste, or $\frac{1}{2}$ teaspoon
Celery: 2 stalks

Boil seasonings in water (about 6 cups). Strain off water and reserve seasonings and water separately for future use. Wash shrimps (leave in jackets) and add to seasoned water and leave in boiling water until shrimps are just cooked – about 3 to 4 minutes. Remove from fire, remove shrimp from water and drain. Keep seasoned water for use later. Chop or slice peppers finely. Peel and clean shrimps and cut lengthwise.

Eggs (hard boiled): 6
Peas and carrots: 1 tin (drain off water)
Sweet pickles (gherkin): 6 sliced or chopped
Olives: 10 sliced
Capers: 1 teaspoon
Salt: to taste or $\frac{1}{4}$ teaspoon
White pepper: generous shake
Mayonnaise: 8 oz (Hellman's or similar)
Seasoned water from shrimp: $\frac{1}{2}$ cup
Gelatin [Davis or other]: $1\frac{1}{2}$ packs dissolved in $\frac{1}{2}$ cup shrimp water
Lettuce or celery leaves: for decoration

Grease food mould or large ring mould generously – preferably with margarine – 2 moulds may be used also. Slice hard boiled eggs, and lay out in moulds. Mix the other ingredients in a large bowl and then pour or lay out in the mould(s). Put in refrigerator until set. Before serving, take mould out of refrigerator and let it stand for a few minutes before turning it over on to the serving dish which can be decorated with lettuce or celery leaves or other attractive decoration. Serve cold.

Crab Backs   Photography by Willie Alleyne. Styling by Jeanine Leemans

Crab Backs

Crab meat (dressed): 1 lb
Onions: 3 small, finely minced
Garlic: 2 cloves, finely minced
Chive and thyme: 1 tablespoon, finely
  minced
Hot pepper: $\frac{1}{2}$, finely minced
Salt and black pepper: to taste, or $\frac{1}{2}$
  teaspoon each
Bread or biscuits: 4 slices or equivalent
Breadcrumbs: 2 handfuls
Corn oil: to sauté
Butter (optional): a pat
Bacon (optional): 2 rashers, finely minced

Sauté onions, garlic, chive and thyme in hot oil. Add crabmeat and then hot pepper, salt and black pepper. Soak bread or biscuits in water, drain off excess water, and add to mixture in pot. Stir, add butter and bacon (if desired), and cook for about 10 minutes, adding a bit of water if necessary to make mixture into a moist consistency. Mix well. Remove pot from heat and let it cool. Fill cleaned crab backs if you have any, or small containers of pyrex or tinfoil, with the mixture. Sprinkle breadcrumbs on top and bake in oven at 350°F for about 15 minutes. Serve hot.

Gérard

When I was in Paris a few years ago, I met Gérard, who was naturally gifted in the culinary arts. He was from Madagascar, of mainly Chinese parentage and a friend of my son. He loved to cook and was the private chef for a wealthy Arabian household. Not only was he an expert in 'La Nouvelle Cuisine', but could prepare superb recipes in Chinese, Vietnamese and Thai cuisines. Our common interest drew us together, and it was not long before he came, by invitation, to spend a week in London, and we cooked every night exquisite, delicious meals.

His versatile skills made him familiar, not only with such recipes as *La Crème Avocat*, *Timbales de Poisson*, *Poisson à la sauce verte* and *Terrine de Champignons*, but he was also equally adept with stuffed chicken wings in a caramel sauce and other Eastern recipes. What attracted me most were the recipes of the Thai cuisine. It seemed to be closer to the West Indian type of cooking using similar herbs, garlic and hot pepper. What I learnt was the use of fresh mint and coriander together, to give unusual, delightful flavours to salads. The following 2 recipes show the application of these herbs with fish sauce in their preparation. Fish sauce is similar to light soy but has a lighter shade and is more suited to seafood dishes. It is obtained at a Chinese grocery.
KAL

Calamari Salad (Squid or Cuttlefish)

Squids (Calamari or Cuttlefish): 1½ lbs, cleaned
Fish sauce (Chinese): 3 tablespoons
Vinegar: 2 teaspoons
Sugar: 1 teaspoon or to taste
Lime juice: 2 teaspoons
Water: 3 tablespoons
Shrimp paste: 1 teaspoon
Fresh coriander: about 4 stalks, chopped
Fresh mint leaves: about 6, chopped
Shallots or chive: 3 blades, chopped
Lettuce: 1 head, shredded
Cucumber: 1, cut lengthwise, 2"
Tomatoes: 4 medium, quartered

Mix lettuce, cucumber and tomatoes with mint, coriander and shallots.

Sauce

Add fish sauce, vinegar, lime juice, water and shrimp paste and mix well together. Keep adding sugar while mixing until dissolved. Some like the tentacles of the squids, many do not, so it is your choice. The main part of the squid is the cylindrical part which is cut and laid flat. Make diagonal criss-crosses into this, but do not cut through completely. Put squids in boiling water for 2 minutes. Put in cold water and drain. Mix the calamari (squids) with the salad. Add the sauce and mix well. Refrigerate before serving cold.

Shrimp Salad with Mint and Coriander

Headless shrimp: 2 lbs, cleaned and
  de-veined
Bean sprouts: 1 lb
Coriander: $\frac{1}{2}$ cup, minced
Mint: $\frac{1}{2}$ cup, chopped
Salt: to taste, or $\frac{1}{2}$ teaspoon
Fish sauce (Chinese): 3 tablespoons
Cabbage: 2 cups, shredded

Cook shrimp in boiling water for 3 minutes. Drain immediately and set aside. Wash and clean bean sprouts. Put in pot of boiling water, cover pot and remove from heat. Let bean sprouts heat soak for 4 minutes. Drain off excess water from the bean sprouts, and mix with the coriander, mint and salt. Lay out on a serving dish. Slice the shrimp lengthwise into halves and arrange in circles, starting from the centre, over the bean sprouts. On the first inner two circles, have the shrimp laid out with the outer surface exposed, and the sliced surface hidden. On the outer circles, have the sliced side of the shrimp exposed. Continue adding circular rows of cut halves of shrimp until the entire dish is covered. Put shredded cabbage at each end of serving dish for decoration. Put in refrigerator and just before serving sprinkle with fish sauce. Serve cold.

Shrimp Salad with Mint and Coriander   Photography by Willie Alleyne. Styling by Marie Henderson

Kitchen Sense

Is it possible to overcome at least some kitchen stress?

With a bit of common sense and thought, most stress circumstances can be avoided or minimised in the kitchen, so that enjoyment is a real possibility during meal preparation. The following guidelines will show how we can set about achieving this goal.

1. Your work counter should ideally cover a 3 foot width, and be positioned near to the kitchen sink and draining board.

2. The work counter should be well lighted, and near a window. If not, the placement of fluorescent lights, fixed to the under surface of the top cupboard above your work counter, will give all the lighting you would need.

3. Items like condiments, soy sauce, etc, and ingredients which are used frequently, should be stored on the work counter in an accessible area. This avoids unnecessary actions of opening and closing the doors, if these items were stored in the cupboards.

The choice of items stored in each drawer should be sensibly rationalised, so that the identity of these items can be recognised easily. For example, one drawer should store the kitchen knives and, if space permits, the potato or carrot peeler, the can opener, and other items that are routinely used. This drawer should be within the work counter.

4. Another drawer will hold kitchen towels and dish cloths, minor baking items, such as spatulas, wooden spoons, whisks, measuring spoons, thermometer gauge, measuring cups. Another drawer will be for cutlery. Other items used infrequently can be stored in a drawer distant from the work area. And so on, so that each drawer is classified according to specific needs, and positioned accordingly. Containers should be labelled for identification of the ingredients they contain – sugar, flour, corn starch, red beans, etc. It is also a good idea to put the date when these items are first stored in the containers.

5. A wax pencil or marker is a durable item for such a purpose, and should be kept handy in the kitchen.

A pad and pencil or pen for taking notes or writing recipes from cook books are also very useful. This way, your cook books do not become smudged unnecessarily.

Labelling and dating of plastic bags or containers storing meats, shrimp and food in the freezer are necessary, or you will run the risk of mixing them up. It is possible to store various items in the freezer and forget about them.

6. The cupboard above your work counter should contain items that you need routinely, for example several small bowls, condiments, a few dishes and other containers that you may need to hold seasonings, vegetables, sliced meats, sauces, etc during the meal preparation.

7. Have a roll of thin polythene film (e.g. glad wrap) at hand for sealing these small bowls when they are used.

Keep one or two chopping boards handy for slicing, mincing, etc small quantities of items. Use a food processor if you have one for larger quantities.

8. Kitchen spoons and spatulas, etc should be hung up at the sink. Pans and pots ideally should be stored on a wooden rack or metal hooks suspended from the ceiling near the stove, or on open wall shelves if that is possible, and not too unattractive.

9. I would prefer to have an entire wall of shelves instead of closed cupboards, as the large dishes and other items stored on open shelves are more readily accessible when needed. An attractive arrangement of wares, etc can contribute to the sense of well-being and enjoyment of those who use the kitchen regularly. As mentioned earlier, storing pots, etc inside cupboards can make access difficult and awkward. *KAL*

Kendal Lee in the kitchen   A family photograph

Poultry

Masquerader in a Carnival costume depicting the Bird of Paradise at the Trinidad Carnival
Courtesy the Trinidad and Tobago Tourist Board

Baked Chicken in Mushroom Sauce

Frying chicken: 3 lbs
Garlic: 2 cloves, minced
Oregano: 1 tablespoon, fresh, or
  1 teaspoon, powdered
Cayenne pepper: 1 teaspoon
Salt: 1 teaspoon
Corn oil: $\frac{1}{4}$ cup
Cheddar cheese: $\frac{1}{2}$ cup, grated

Cut chicken into pieces. Season with salt, pepper, garlic and oregano. Let stand for 1 hour. Sauté in corn oil, turning to brown on all sides. Remove and place on a baking dish.

Mushroom Sauce

Butter: 2 tablespoons
Flour: 3 tablespoons
Milk: 1 cup
White wine: 1 cup
Mushrooms, canned: 1 cup, sliced
Onions: $\frac{1}{2}$ cup, minced
Salt: $\frac{1}{2}$ teaspoon
Parsley: 1 tablespoon, finely minced

Melt butter in a saucepan at low medium heat. Sauté the onions until glazed. Add salt, milk and wine, stirring constantly until it is blended well. Add mushrooms and parsley, mixing well. Pour entire contents over the chicken, cover with grated cheese and bake in oven at 325°F for 45 minutes.

Baked Chicken in a Herbal Tomato Sauce

Chicken: 3½ lbs, cut into bite-size pieces
Garlic: 2 cloves, minced
Black pepper and salt: 1 teaspoon each
Sherry: 1 tablespoon
Corn oil: ¼ cup

Season chicken with garlic, salt, pepper and sherry. Set aside for 1 hour.
Heat oil in a heavy pot and sauté chicken pieces until browned. Drain pieces and put on a baking dish.

Herbal Tomato Sauce

Tomato sauce: 1 cup
Basil leaves: 1 tablespoon, minced or
   1 teaspoon, powdered
Tomato paste: 1 tablespoon
Worcester sauce: 2 teaspoons
Onion: 1 medium, minced
Celery: 1 tablespoon, minced
Stock: 1 cup – chicken
Salt: ½ teaspoon
Butter: 2 tablespoons
Flour: 1 tablespoon

In a saucepan, melt butter and sauté onions until glazed. Add flour and stir until blended. Add rest of ingredients and cook over low heat until sauce is thickened. Pour sauce over chicken in baking dish and bake in moderate oven (350°F) for 35 minutes. Serve hot.

Braised Chicken Breasts in a Tarragon Cream Sauce

Chicken breasts: 3, boned
Salt: ½ teaspoon
Tarragon: 2 teaspoons
White pepper: 1 teaspoon
Clarified butter (see recipe): 4 tablespoons
Sour cream: ½ cup
Stock: 2 cups, chicken
Onions: ½ cup, minced
Cognac: 2 tablespoons

Place chicken breasts between 2 sheets of waxed paper. Flatten the fillet with a wooden kitchen mallet, or the side of a cleaver, to a thickness of ½″. Cut each fillet into 2 or 3 pieces. Season with salt, tarragon and pepper. Set aside for 1 hour. In a saucepan, bring to boil the stock and the onions, and cook until volume is reduced by half. Add in the sour cream. Sauté the chicken breasts in a separate heated pot, using clarified butter, until browned and cooked. Flambé the cognac and pour it over the chicken. Continue cooking until the cognac is absorbed. Add sour cream and blend for one minute. Transfer to serving dish and serve hot.

Caribbean Chicken Stew

Here, the meats are browned by the sugar burnt in hot oil (caramelizing the sugar). When sugar is cooked in hot oil, it turns brown and the meat is then sautéed to give a rich brown colour, varying in tone according to how long the sugar is burnt. This browning method gives a distinctive flavour to West Indian stews.

Various herbs are grown on the foothills of Maraval in Trinidad where Paramin Village is located. These villagers are descendants of French extract, and patois is still spoken by the older residents. There, the drainage is excellent for growing herbs, with a good distribution of rain and sun. The herbs are sold in the local market in assorted bunches – thyme, chive, oregano, celery, parsley, fennel and others.

Chicken: 3–4 lbs, whole
Garlic: 3 cloves, minced
Maraval herbs – chive, thyme, etc: $\frac{1}{2}$ cup, finely minced
Rum, Trinidad or Barbados: 2 fluid oz
Sugar: 1 tablespoon, brown
Vinegar: 1 tablespoon
Salt: 1 teaspoon
Hot pepper: 1 teaspoon, minced
Corn oil: $\frac{1}{4}$ cup
Cornstarch: 2 teaspoons

Cut chicken into stewing pieces. Mix ingredients together and season the chicken well. Let it marinate for an hour. Heat oil to high temperature in a heavy (preferably) iron pot. Add a tablespoon of brown sugar to caramelize. When sugar is a rich brown colour, add the chicken pieces, turning frequently so all sides are browned.

When chicken is well browned, reduce heat to medium; add the rest of the marinade, and 2 cups of water. Cover pot and let cook for 40 minutes, stirring from time to time. Just before it is done, add 2 teaspoons cornstarch dissolved in 1 tablespoon of water to chicken. Stir to thicken. Serve hot.

Boiled Chicken in Ginger Sauce

Chicken: 1 whole, about 3 lbs
Chive: 1 cup, chopped
Ginger: 6 slices, cut in strips
Sesame oil: 2 teaspoons
Corn oil: 2 tablespoons
Soy sauce (light): 3 teaspoons
Salt and pepper: to taste

Immerse chicken into a pot of boiling salted water. Simmer gently for 30 to 40 minutes. Transfer chicken to plate and let cool. Cut up chicken into bite-size pieces and return to serving dish.

In frying pan, heat both oils together. When hot and smoking, put chive and ginger into pan, adding a dash of salt and pepper. Stir a few times, remove from heat and add soy sauce. Pour sauce over chicken and blend well. Serve hot or cold – preferably hot.

Chicken in Batter with Carrots and Peppers

Chicken breast: 1 lb, boned and cut into 1″
  pieces
Garlic: 1 clove, minced
Root ginger: 12 slices, cut into thin strips
Chive or scallions: 2 blades, minced
Carrot: 1 medium, cut into 1″ × ½″ pieces
Sweet (Bell) peppers: 2, cut into 1″ pieces
Corn oil: to deep fry

Sauce

Stock: ¼ cup (chicken)
Sherry: 1 tablespoon
Light soy sauce: 1 tablespoon
Tomato paste: 1 tablespoon
Cornstarch: 2 teaspoons

Batter

Egg whites: 2
Cornstarch: 1 tablespoon
Water: 2 or more teaspoons
Salt: 1 teaspoon
Sesame oil: a few drops

Mix sauce ingredients together in a bowl.
Dip chicken pieces in batter and deep fry
in oil until golden. Remove and drain.
Pour off excess oil, leaving about 2 tablespoons. Stir-fry ginger, garlic, scallions,
peppers and carrots for a minute. Add the
chicken to pot with 1 tablespoon of water.
Cover to steam-fry for one minute. Add
the sauce mixture and blend well until
sauce is thickened.
Arrange on serving dish and sprinkle with
sesame oil and serve hot.

Fried Chicken (Chinese Style)

Whole chicken: 1–3½ lbs cleaned
Light soy sauce: 2 tablespoons
Spice powder: 1 tablespoon
Rum (Trinidad or Barbados): 2
  tablespoons
Garlic: 1 clove, minced
Black pepper: 1 teaspoon
Salt: ½ teaspoon
Sesame oil: 1 teaspoon
Corn oil: to deep fry

Immerse chicken in a pot of boiling water
for 15 minutes. Remove, drain and dry
chicken thoroughly.
Season chicken, rubbing seasonings inside
and outside thoroughly and let stand for
an hour.
Deep fry over moderate fire until golden
brown. Drain and remove. Cut into bite-
size pieces and arrange on a serving dish
neatly. Garnish with 1 tablespoon of chopped chives and serve hot.

Chicken Casserole in a Melongene Tomato Sauce

Chicken: 3½ lbs
Salt and pepper: to taste or 1 teaspoon each
Garlic: 2 cloves, minced
Fresh or dried thyme: 1 tablespoon, minced or 1 teaspoon, dried
Onion: 1 cup, minced
Melongene: 1 large
Stock: 1 cup (chicken)
Tomato paste: 2 tablespoons
Worcester sauce: 1 tablespoon
Sugar: 2 teaspoons
Green (Bell) peppers: 2, sliced
Corn oil: 4 tablespoons

Cut up chicken in bite-size pieces, season with garlic, salt and pepper to taste.
Sauté peppers in hot oil for 30 seconds, drain and set aside on to a dish.
Then put chicken in casserole pot and sauté until browned. Remove chicken pieces to platter. Pare and cut the melongene into 2″ pieces; heat the melongene in a separate pot with ¼ cup water, and cook slowly until it is soft. Blend together by stirring. Put the stock in casserole pot with tomato paste, thyme, Worcester sauce, sugar and 1 cup of the melongene purée, and cook slowly, stirring until blended. Put back the chicken pieces, cover and continue to cook for 35 minutes. Add salt to correct sauce if necessary. Put on serving dish and garnish with the green peppers. Serve hot.

Lime Chicken

Chicken breasts: 2 whole, boned and cut into bite-size pieces
Root ginger: 1 piece, thumb-size cut into thin strips
Salt: ¼ teaspoon
Black pepper: a shake, or to taste
Lime peel: 1 lime peel, thinly sliced
Lime juice: ¼ cup (from 3 limes)
Limes: 2 sliced for garnish
Stock – chicken: 1 cup
Sugar: ½ cup
Egg yolk: 1
Corn oil: 2 tablespoons

Batter Mix

Flour: 5 tablespoons
Cornstarch: 2 tablespoons
Baking powder: ¼ teaspoon
Water: to make a creamy paste

Mix batter ingredients with just enough water to make a creamy paste. Season bite-size pieces of chicken breasts with salt and pepper. Dip and drench each piece with the batter mix. Deep fry chicken pieces until golden brown in colour. Drain and put on a serving dish.
Heat 2 tablespoons of corn oil in a frying pan and sauté shredded ginger and lime rind. Pour in lime juice, stock and sugar and cook for two minutes. Thicken sauce with cornstarch liquid (2 teaspoons cornstarch dissolved in 2 tablespoons water) and remove from heat. Beat egg yolk and add to lime sauce, stirring rapidly until egg is completely blended in sauce. This must be done quickly or egg yolk will curdle in the sauce. Pour sauce over chicken and garnish with thin half slices of lime.

Krispy Chicken

Chicken: 1 whole, 3–4 lbs
Honey: 2 tablespoons
Onions or shallots: 1 cup, minced
Soy sauce (light): 1 tablespoon
Chicken or pork stock: enough to immerse
   chicken in pot – about 10 cups
Corn oil: same amount as stock

Immerse chicken in a pot of boiling stock so that it is completely covered. Put honey, minced onions or shallots and soy sauce into stock. Cover and cook over low heat for 30 minutes. Remove chicken and suspend it with a hook for 3 hours until liquid has drained off and it is absolutely dry.

However, there is another way to achieve this 'dried out' result. After removing chicken from pot and draining off as much liquid as possible, place it on a rack which is placed over a dish and store it in a frost-free refrigerator for several hours (4–5) or overnight. The frost-free action of the refrigerator will dry out all the moisture and give the desired effect.

Heat oil to boiling in a deep fryer and immerse chicken in the hot oil and cook until it is honey-coloured. Drain off excess oil and place chicken on a rack to dry out for ½ hour. Cut chicken into serving portions. The skin will be crisp and the meat succulent and tasty. It may be seasoned with seasoned salt.

Seasoned Salt

Salt: 1 tablespoon
Chinese spice powder: 2 tablespoons
Black pepper: ½ teaspoon

Put all ingredients in a heated saucepan for 3 minutes. Put in a small bowl and serve with chicken.

Lime Chicken   Photography by Willie Alleyne. Styling by Marie Henderson

Chicken and Pigeon Peas

Chicken, cut into stewing pieces: $3\frac{1}{2}$ lbs
Vinegar: 2 teaspoons
Garlic: 2 cloves, minced
Celery: 1 tablespoon, chopped
Chive: 2 tablespoons, chopped
Salt: 1 teaspoon
Black pepper: $\frac{1}{2}$ teaspoon
Rum (Trinidad or Barbados): 2 tablespoons
Brown sugar: 2 teaspoons
Pigeon peas: 1 lb when shelled
Corn oil: $\frac{1}{4}$ cup
Cornstarch or St Vincent arrowroot: 2 teaspoons
Water: 2 tablespoons

Season chicken with vinegar, rum, celery, chive, salt, black pepper and garlic. Marinate for 1 hour.

Boil pigeon peas in salted water for about 30 minutes or until almost tender. Drain and set aside.

Heat oil in iron skillet or pot and, when hot, add sugar to caramelize. When brown, add chicken pieces and stir pot until pieces have been browned to a honeyed colour.

When all the moisture has evaporated, add the rest of the marinade contents and the drained cooked pigeon peas. Add enough water to almost cover the contents, cover and cook until liquid is reduced to one third, or until chicken is cooked, about 35 to 40 minutes.

Correct flavour of sauce with salt if necessary. Add cornstarch dissolved in water to thicken sauce.

Transfer to dish and serve hot.

Chicken and Pigeon Peas

Photography by Willie Alleyne. Styling by Marie Henderson

Gloria

I met Gloria Chu in 1974 in Trinidad where she had opened and managed a Chinese restaurant. I learnt that she was from New York, and was a restaurant consultant, and had recently sold her successful Chinese restaurant in New Jersey. Her desire for adventure and change to seek new pastures brought her to this assigment in Trinidad.

We became friends, and I soon found out that she was gifted in every aspect of restaurant business. She was the 'complete' restaurant consultant. Apart from her culinary skills, she had the ability to motivate the staff in the right direction. They were devoted to her in spite of her discipline, and gave of their services willingly and efficiently. She substituted local vegetables and fruits that were available and plentiful, such as tamarind, christophene, and topi tamboo. She found out that mussels were in abundance in Trinidad, and were little used or known as an edible seafood. Gloria made mussels a very popular dish on her menu, and now they are well known and enjoyed. In short, she made her mark in the restaurant business in Trinidad.

She brought elegance to the restaurant with her gracious appearance and charm. She returned to New York in 1975.

Fame was the ultimate reward to come to Gloria. She has subsequently established a few restaurants that are outstanding successes. Articles and columns of her successes have appeared in the *Gourmet* and *New York* magazines, and the *Zagat New York City Restaurant Survey*.

In 1985 Gloria received the Omega Mark of Achievement Award for her outstanding abilities and performance in her field.

My co-author, Errol Barrow, had become her friend also, and as a gesture, we invited her to Barbados to renew our friendship and she prepared recipes for this book. Having lived in the West Indies for a few years, it is fitting that some of her famous recipes should be included.
KAL

Poached Soy Sauce Chicken　　　Photography by Willie Alleyne. Styling by Eleanor Chandler

Poached Soy Sauce Chicken

Fresh chicken: 1, whole, not frozen
Light soy sauce: 6 cups
Dark soy sauce: 2 cups
Gin or sherry: 2 cups
Sugar: 8 oz
Root ginger: 1 thumb, peeled
Scallions or chive: 1 bunch (8 to 10 blades)
Garlic: 5 cloves, crushed
Sesame oil: 2 tablespoons
Star anise: 4
Whole nutmeg: 1, grated
Cinnamon: 4 sticks
Peppercorns: 4 teaspoons
or *Black pepper:* 1 teaspoon
Whole cloves: 1 teaspoon
Fennel seeds: 2 teaspoons
Put above 6 spices in muslin bag
Soup stock or water: 8 cups

Put all the ingredients, except the chicken, in a stock pot large enough to hold the ingredients and the chicken. Bring the contents of the pot to a boil, then slow simmer for a least 30 minutes.

Wash and towel dry the chicken. Place it in the pot with other ingredients that have been boiled, and poach the chicken on a slow simmer (do not let it fast boil) until the juice runs clean when the chicken is pierced between thigh and breast meat (not more than 45 minutes).

Turn off heat, and let stand a few minutes more. Remove and cut into serving pieces and add some sauce from stock pot to the chicken.

May be eaten hot or at room temperature.

Pork may be used in place of the chicken. Make sure the stock pot is large enough to hold the pork and not let the sauce boil over. Pork has to be well cooked, and will take longer than a chicken to be well done.

Roast Chicken with Spicy Stuffing

Roasting chicken: about 3½ lbs whole
Soy sauce: 2 tablespoons
Salt: to taste
Black pepper, freshly ground: to taste
Garlic: 1 clove, minced
Poultry stuffing (see recipe)

Season chicken inside and out with soy sauce, garlic, salt and black pepper.

The flavour of a roasted chicken depends to a large measure on the quality of a well seasoned stuffing. This stuffing is the best I have ever tasted, and all credit goes to my wife, Ave, for this outstanding recipe. It is so good that she is constantly asked to prepare this stuffing for family and friends. (See *Poultry stuffing* recipe.)

Prepare poultry stuffing and stuff cavity of the bird with this stuffing, using skewers to hold the stuffing in place. Put stuffed chicken in baking dish, add 1 cup of water to pan. Cover with tin foil and bake in an oven heated to 325°F for 1½ hours. Remove tin foil 45 minutes before completed time so chicken will brown to a golden colour. Baste with drippings. Remove to a serving dish. Add water to drippings and blend. Thicken with 1 teaspoon cornstarch dissolved in 1 tablespoon of water, and serve gravy separately.

Poultry Stuffing

Bread: 6 slices, soaked in a little water
Breadcrumbs: 1 cup
Raisins: 1 cup
Olives (stuffed): 6 sliced
Capers: 6
Onions: 2–3 small, diced
Garlic: 2–3 cloves, minced
Chive: ½ cup, chopped
Thyme – fresh: 1 tablespoon, freshly chopped
Hot pepper: to taste or 1–2
Salt: to taste or about ½ teaspoon
Black pepper: to taste
Bacon: 4–5 slices, finely chopped
Ham or sausage meat: ½ lb chopped
Chicken livers: 4–5, finely chopped
Corn oil, or similar type: 2 tablespoons, or as desired

Heat oil in frying pan, brown garlic, onions, then add chive and thyme. Add bacon, ham (or sausage meat), and chicken livers. These meats may be browned separately in another pan if so desired before adding to seasonings. Add bread, raisins, olives, capers, hot pepper (finely cut up), salt and black pepper. Add a little water if the mixture is too dry, and let cook on medium to low heat for about 20 minutes. Add breadcrumbs and turn off heat. This stuffing may be put in a chicken or turkey before baking, or may be baked in a dish in the oven, with breadcrumbs sprinkled on top, for about 30 minutes. Serve hot – gives about 6 good servings.

Shredded Chicken with Chinese Vegetables Photography by Willie Alleyne. Styling by Jeanine Leemans

Shredded Chicken with Chinese Vegetables

Here the Chinese vegetables used are *wah-nee* (wooden ears) and dried mushrooms which can be obtained at a Chinese grocery. These are listed in the glossary for further information.

Chicken breast: $\frac{1}{2}$ lb
Chinese mushrooms (dried): 6, soaked and thinly sliced
Wah-nee: a handful, soaked
Salt: 1 teaspoon
Cornstarch: 1 teaspoon
Light soy: 2 tablespoons
Rum (Trinidad or Barbados): 1 tablespoon
Scallions or chive: 3 tablespoons, chopped
Root ginger: 2 slices, cut into thin strips
Garlic: 1 clove, minced
Oyster sauce: 1 tablespoon
Sugar: 2 teaspoons
Lime juice: 2 teaspoons (from peeled limes)
Corn oil: 3 tablespoons

Cut chicken breast into $1\frac{1}{2}''$ strips (matchstick size). Mix with salt and cornstarch. Soak *wah-nee* and mushrooms in bowl of warm water for 20 minutes. Drain and remove. Cut *wah-nee* and mushrooms into smaller pieces. Heat oil and sauté garlic, ginger and scallions for $\frac{1}{2}$ minute.
Add chicken, and stir-fry until excess liquid is evaporated. Add the Chinese vegetables (mushrooms and *wah-nee*), soy sauce, sugar, rum, lime juice and oyster sauce. Cook for 8 minutes; add 1 teaspoon cornstarch dissolved in 1 tablespoon water to thicken sauce. Blend well and serve hot.

Steam-Grilled Chicken

Chicken: 3 to 4 lbs, quartered
Dark soy sauce: 2 teaspoons
Garlic: 1 large clove, crushed and minced
Sherry: 1 tablespoon
Salt: $\frac{1}{2}$ teaspoon
Black pepper: $\frac{1}{2}$ teaspoon
Cornstarch: 1 teaspoon

Cut chicken into quartered sections. Season with all ingredients and let it marinate for 2 hours.
In a grilling pan, place chicken parts on the rack. Add 1 cup of water at bottom of pan together with any marinade contents left over. Set oven at broil temperature and pre-heat oven for 10 minutes. Place the grill pan with the chicken portions at the bottom level of oven and grill for approximately 35 minutes or until both sides of the chicken portions are golden in colour. Turn each part over after one side is browned. The combination of the steaming from the marinade stock and grilling will give the golden grilled chicken a tender succulent taste.

Steamed Chicken

Plump chicken (whole): 1, 3 to 3½ lbs
Chives or scallions: 1 blade, chopped
Garlic: 2 cloves, chopped
Root ginger: 1 'thumb', chopped
Salt and black pepper: to taste
Cooking oil: a bit
Rum (Trinidad or Barbados): a dash
Chinese oyster sauce: 1 teaspoon
Sugar: a bit
Cornstarch: 1 teaspoon

Clean chicken thoroughly. Sprinkle a little salt in inside and on outside. Rub outside of chicken with some cooking oil, to give it a glossy colour. Have the water boiling in a steaming pot before putting the chicken into a dish inside the pot. Cover and let steam for about 30 to 40 minutes, depending on the size of the chicken. Steam must not be too intense, or the meat on the legs will tend to break or separate.

At the end of the cooking time, you can pierce the joint by the thigh with a fork, and if the liquid is not pink, then it is done. Let the chicken cool before cutting it into small pieces, and put into a serving dish. Sprinkle top with chopped chives.

In a saucepan, heat some oil and, when sizzling hot, add chopped garlic and ginger. Add some of the stock from the steamed chicken, a dash of rum, a little bit of oyster sauce, a dash of sugar, salt to taste, and cornstarch dissolved in water, to thicken sauce. Then pour over the entire dish of steamed chicken.

The garlic and ginger may be removed from the hot oil before adding the stock and the other ingredients, but many like the taste of these ingredients. Serve hot or cold.

Stuffed Chicken Wings with a Caramel Sauce

Chicken wings: 10 boned
Minced chicken: ¾ cup
Minced pork: ⅓ cup
Soy sauce: 1 tablespoon
Chinese dried mushrooms: 5
Chives or scallions: 2 tablespoons, chopped
Sesame oil: 1 teaspoon
Cornstarch: 1 teaspoon

Break off the wing tips and bone the chicken wings (see below).

Soak mushrooms in hot water for 20 minutes, drain in cold water and cut off stems. Mince the mushrooms. The chicken and pork can be minced in a food processor if you have one. Mix all the ingredients together and stuff the chicken wings Seal the exposed ends with the skins. Line a baking tray with tin foil and spread some oil to smear the tin foil. Lay the wings on the tin foil and bake for 40 minutes in the oven set at 350°F. When completed, lay out wings on a serving dish.

Boning chicken wings:

Boning wings is a bit tedious and time-consuming, and this recipe is suited for only those who really enjoy cooking, and have the time and patience to do so.

If you think this is difficult, try boning a whole chicken without cutting the skin or outer surface. I have done so on several occasions.

With a sharp knife, cut around the head of the bone that separates the wing from the body, severing the tendons. With the blade of the knife, scrape the meat along the length of the bone until it reaches the joint, turning back the skin and meat over un-boned portion like a glove. Cut through the tendons and gently peel around the joint carefully using the side of the blade to expose the joint. Break the two smaller bones as they leave the joint with the back of a heavy knife. Peel away the rest of the meat from the two smaller bones and twist them off the joint at the wing tip. Fold back the meat to assume its proper shape.

Caramel Sauce

Granulated sugar: 6 oz
Water: $\frac{3}{4}$ pint

In a heavy saucepan, melt 4 ounces of sugar slowly. When it is bubbly and brown in colour, add the water. It will fizz dangerously, so be careful of spattering. Add the rest of the sugar and bring to boiling until it is of a syrup consistency. Pour over chicken wings and serve hot.

Stuffed Chicken Wings with a Caramel Sauce
Photography by Willie Alleyne. Styling by Marie Henderson

Home Made Mayonnaise Salad (Chicken, Shrimp or Fish)

Chicken: about 2 lbs, breast, leg and thighs
OR *Shrimp:* about 40 medium
OR *Fish:* 2 lbs, Carite, King, or similar, steamed and flaked
OR *Lobster:* about 2, boiled and cut in chunks
Eggs: 6 (4 hard boiled)
Oil, corn: about ½ pint
Salt, black pepper: to taste
Capers: 1 teaspoon
Stuffed olives: 4 sliced
Garlic: 1 clove, finely minced
Vinegar, white or lime juice: a few drops

Boil chicken (or shrimp, etc), cool and take out bones, then strip or cut into small bits. Separate egg yolks and put away the whites. Put yolks in a shallow bowl, and using a fork, add oil very slowly to the yolks – a few drops at a time. Turn the

Home Made Mayonnaise Salad—Shrimp
Photography by Willie Alleyne. Styling by Marie Henderson

fork in the mixture until it is well blended and firm. If mixture curdles, you can either
1) Use another egg yolk or
2) Use a teaspoon of prepared mayonnaise (Hellman's, French's, etc) to start over again. Be sure to put in only a few drops of oil at a time, as too much oil at a time can be the cause of the mixture curdling. When the new mixture is firm, you can add in the curdled mixture, bit by bit, and more oil will be needed. You will now have about double the amount of mayonnaise sauce, some of which can be stored in the refrigerator for a few days for future use.
When mixture is firm, add salt, black pepper and minced garlic to taste, then capers and olives. Cut up hard boiled eggs in small chunks and mix with mayonnaise dressing; add stripped chicken (or shrimp, etc), leaving a bit of mayonnaise aside for the potato salad.

Salad

Carrots: 2, boiled, peeled and sliced
Garden peas: 1 tin, drained of water or 1 tin of peas and carrots
Potatoes: 6 medium, boiled, and peeled
Onions: 1 small, grated
Lettuce: 1 head, washed clean
Tomatoes: 4 firm, medium, sliced
Mayonnaise, home made or prepared: about 4 oz
Celery: 1 stalk
Salt and black pepper: to taste

Dice boiled potatoes and add grated onion to taste, then add about 2 tablespoons mayonnaise, salt and black pepper. Mix in a large bowl. Separate washed lettuce leaves, and arrange around the edge of a large serving platter or dish. Arrange sliced tomatoes on top of lettuce, then garden peas, leaving space in the centre for chicken (or shrimp, etc) mayonnaise mixture. Arrange sliced carrots around edge of mayonnaise mixture, and decorate the centre with lettuce or celery. Refrigerate and serve cold.

Stuffed Chicken Legs
Photography by Willie Alleyne. Styling by Marie Henderson

Stuffed Chicken Legs

Chicken: 4 legs and thighs, unjointed and boned
Dark soy sauce: 2 teaspoons
Sherry: 1 tablespoon
Salt: $\frac{1}{2}$ teaspoon
Black pepper: $\frac{1}{2}$ teaspoon
Cornstarch: 2 teaspoons
Onion: 1 medium, chopped
Fresh ginger: 1 piece, thumb-size, cut into thin strips
Chicken stock: 1 cup

Deboning the chicken legs and thighs:
At the open end of the thigh, cut through the tendons and gently separate the meat from the bone with a small sharp kitchen knife until the thigh bone is fully exposed to where it is jointed to the leg. Continue separating the bone by cutting through the tendons around the joint and along the length of the bone. Remove the meat completely from the bone and set aside.
In a bowl, mix the dark soy, sherry, salt and pepper and cornstarch into a thin paste. Spoon the paste into the cavities of the boned parts.

Stuffing

Carrot: 1, cleaned and cut into 12 long strips – julienne
Chive or scallions: 4 stalks
Ripe plantain: 4 long strips, peeled
Cabbage leaves: 4

On each cabbage leaf, place 2–3 strips of carrot, 1 stalk of chive and 1 strip of plantain. Fold the cabbage leaf to enclose them and form a roll.
Fill each cavity of the deboned chicken parts with a stuffed cabbage roll. Fold over the exposed portion of the thigh with the loose chicken skin. Tie the leg at intervals with kitchen thread so it appears elongated as a sausage.
Heat oil in pot and sauté the onions and ginger for a minute. Put in the chicken portions and brown. Then add stock, cover and cook on low heat for 35 minutes. Remove legs from pot on to a platter. Remove strings from legs and cut diagonally in 1″ cross-sectional pieces.
Arrange pieces on serving dish, pour sauce over them, and serve hot.

Kitchen Plan

Kitchen lovers, what image do you have of your ideal kitchen? I see the kitchen as the focal centre of interest, around which other rooms in the house are supportive to it.

The kitchen is the room where you should be able to go after a tense working day, to relax, get a drink, have a snack, have a chat with your spouse or other household members, and generally restore your mental equilibrium. I see the kitchen as a stage on which you, the kitchen lover, perform before your 'captive' audience – your friends and guests – and orchestrate the cooking of the meal.

Over the years, I have been instrumental in designing several kitchens in homes, but there was one which incorporated the ideas I had. The kitchen was in the home of an architect who appreciated the thoughts I had, and had the courage to implement them.

The area of 14 feet by 12 feet minimum was adequate for my purpose, and it was set, as it were, on a platform, 14 inches above the floor, overlooking the living area. An island work-counter area $3\frac{1}{2}$ by 6 feet, set in the centre of the kitchen, provided the focal point for the preparation and cooking of the meal. On this island work area, a built-in surface range, small sink and a covered circular opening for disposal of waste into the bin underneath were featured. Overhead hung the kitchen spoons and there were additional spot lights for illumination.

Three-foot traffic spaces separated supportive working counters and storage cupboards which were fixed on the walls where space permitted. There were no overhead cupboards to obstruct the view between kitchen and other daytime areas such as the living room.

The effect was to simulate a stage-like appearance. On the far wall behind the island, facing the living area, was a series of shelves on which colourful pots and dishes were arranged attractively. These, by careful placement, gave a colourful backdrop for the kitchen stage.

In this manner, the host cook can become the performer on stage facing his guest audience, and demonstrate his culinary skills.

If you have a large family, or find your kitchen space is inadequate for your needs, resurrecting the idea of the pantry of yesteryear could easily be included in another room adjacent to the kitchen. In the pantry area, additional storage for foods, kitchen accessories, including the extra dishes and pots used only occasionally, and even a freezer, can be located.

Having a large sink for cleaning and scouring of pots could avoid unnecessary clutter and traffic in your kitchen. Thus the pantry, if included, could relieve the kitchen of overcrowding of stored items and ingredients, and make it a more suitable environment for enjoyable cooking.

Another suggestion for relieving the kitchen of storage, would be to have a walk-in food storage cupboard. Shelves lining the walls from floor to ceiling will store not only canned foods and liquid seasonings, but also additional pots and dishes.

These thoughts I have thrust upon you, as a result of the wealth of experiences I have collected over the years of my love of cooking. My aim is to make the task of preparing food, which is vital to satisfy one of the most essential functions of man

Bottom Bay, St Philip, Barbados

Photography by Willie Alleyne

– eating – as enjoyable, interesting and satisfying as I have experienced. Perhaps, in my later writings, I can enlarge on my theme of sensuous cooking, and how to become a sensuous cook.

KAL

Lion at Gun Hill, St George, Barbados

Photography by Willie Alleyne

52

Beef

Beef and Melongene in Hot Sauce

Beef tenderloin: 12 oz, shredded
Chive: 2 stalks, finely minced
Root ginger: 3 slices, finely chopped
Garlic: 1 clove, finely chopped
Soy sauce: 1 tablespoon
Rum (Trinidad or Barbados): 1 tablespoon
Sugar: 1 teaspoon
Cornstarch (St Vincent arrowroot): $1\frac{1}{2}$ teaspoons
Melongene (egg plant, aubergine): 1 medium, peeled and cut into 1″ pieces
Hot pepper sauce (see recipe): 1 teaspoon
Stock (beef, chicken or pork): $\frac{1}{2}$ cup
Corn oil: $\frac{1}{2}$ cup

Mix chive, ginger, soy sauce, garlic, rum and cornstarch with beef. Marinate for 1 hour. Heat oil in pot and quick fry the melongene. Drain and remove to a dish. Pour off all except 1 tablespoon of the oil from the pot. Sauté beef in pot for 2 minutes. Add melongene, hot sauce, sugar and stock. Cook until stock liquid is reduced to half the volume. Serve hot.

Beef Curry in Coconut Milk

Stewing beef: 2 lbs, cut into 1″ pieces
Garlic: 2 cloves, minced
Onions: 1 cup, minced
Curry powder: 4 tablespoons
Lime juice: 2 teaspoons
Sugar: 1 teaspoon
Coconut milk (see recipe): 1 cup
Water: 1 cup
Corn oil: 4 tablespoons
Salt and black pepper: to taste or $\frac{1}{2}$ teaspoon each

Heat oil in a pan. Add 2 tablespoons curry powder and, when bubbly, add meat to brown. Add onions and garlic and cook for 2 to 3 minutes. Add rest of ingredients. Cover pan; cook over low to medium heat for 1 hour, stirring meat frequently. Serve hot with white rice. This recipe may be used to make chicken or shrimp curry also. The cooking time for these substitutions will be less – 30 minutes for chicken and 5 minutes for shrimp.

Calypso 'Birds'

Beef, rump or topside: 2½ lbs
Salt and black pepper: to taste or ½ teaspoon each
Boiled spinach: 2 cups, squeezed to a pulpy texture
Bacon: 3 rashers, chopped
Onions: ½ cup, minced
Tomato paste: 1 teaspoon
Breadcrumbs: ½ cup
Thyme: 1 sprig, minced
Stock (beef): 1 cup
Rum (Barbados or Trinidad): 1 fluid oz

Cut beef into thin slices 4″ × 2½″, flattening with wooden mallet if necessary to have them uniformly thin. Combine together in a bowl, the spinach, bacon, thyme, tomato paste, onions, breadcrumbs and any left over beef trimmings (cut up these beef trimmings). Add salt and black pepper to make a stuffing mixture.

Place some of the stuffing on each slice. Roll up each slice and tie it with a string or thread.

Heat up oil in a pan, and brown each roll on all sides. Drain off excess oil from pan and add stock and rum. Cover the pan and cook at low heat for an hour, or until the 'birds' are tender.

Taste for additional salt and black pepper; thicken gravy with 1 teaspoon cornstarch dissolved in 1 tablespoon of water. Lay out 'birds' in rows on a platter, remove string; serve gravy in separate gravy boat. Serve hot.

Caribbean Steak Tartare

Beef tenderloin: 1 lb, finely chopped
Salt: ½ teaspoon
Black pepper: 1 teaspoon, freshly ground
Worcester sauce: 1 tablespoon
Chive or shallots: 2 tablespoons, finely minced
Celery: 1 tablespoon, finely chopped
Parsley: 1 tablespoon, finely chopped
Smoked herring seasoning (see recipe): ½ teaspoon, optional
Capers: 1 tablespoon
Black olives: 1 tablespoon, chopped
Egg yolk: 1
Onion: 1, medium, finely chopped

The meat must be of good quality.
Mix all ingredients well together. Form into patties and serve.

Steak Creole

Steaks – rib eye or sirloin: 6, 1" thick
Chive: 2 tablespoons, chopped
Thyme: 1 sprig, minced
Rum (Barbados or Trinidad): 1 fluid oz
Beef stock or consommé: $\frac{1}{2}$ cup
Butter: 4 tablespoons
Worcester sauce: 1 tablespoon
Salt and black pepper: to taste or $\frac{1}{4}$
    teaspoon each
Cornstarch (arrowroot): $\frac{1}{2}$ teaspoon

Put butter in a heavy skillet over moderate heat. When the butter has foamed and begins to subside, it is right for the steaks.

Cook steaks in butter, 2 at a time, turning frequently for approximately 4 minutes until medium rare. Test a steak by cutting a small incision in it. When correctly cooked, remove to a platter, keep warm, and continue to cook in the same way until all the steaks are done. Put all cooked steaks into the skillet. Season with salt and black pepper. Add chive, thyme, and sauté for 1 minute. Then add stock, rum, Worcester sauce and sugar and cook over low medium heat, scraping up brown congealed bits from bottom of pan. Add more salt if desired and cook until syrupy. Thicken sauce with $\frac{1}{2}$ teaspoon cornstarch dissolved in 1 tablespoon of water. Pour sauce over steak and serve hot.

The Scarlet Ibis in flight at the Caroni Bird Sanctuary, Trinidad
Courtesy the Trinidad and Tobago Tourist Board

Pot Roast Claudette

This is an excellent way of cooking a pot roast, simmering slowly in the combined juices of the meat and onions. If done this way, neither water nor stock need be added. But care should be taken to keep the heat very low so that there will be minimal evaporation of the cooking liquids.

Rump of beef or topside: 4 to 5 lbs
Garlic: 2 cloves, minced
Salt and black pepper: to taste or 1 teaspoon
Worcester sauce: 1 tablespoon
Onions: 3 cups, chopped
Tomato sauce: $\frac{1}{2}$ cup
Sugar: 2 teaspoons
Thyme (fresh): 2 sprigs
Bayleaf: 1
Rum (Barbados or Trinidad): $1\frac{1}{2}$ fluid oz
Corn oil: 3 tablespoons

Season meat with salt, pepper and Worcester sauce. Heat oil in a large pot and brown meat on all sides. Remove browned meat and place on a platter. Into the large pot, put in onions, garlic, tomato sauce, bay leaf, thyme, sugar and rum. Lay the meat gently on this bed of onions, etc. Cover pot, and simmer slowly for $1\frac{1}{4}$ hours until meat is tender. If the cooking liquid formed from the meat and onion juices is evaporating too quickly, add a small amount of water. Remove meat on to a large dish and pour blended gravy into a sauce boat. Serve hot.

Jug or Jug Jug

Very Barbadian dish popular at Christmas time. Served with traditional Christmas dishes such as boiled ham and roasted pork.

Dry pigeon peas: 2 lbs
Stew beef: 1 lb
Salt beef: $\frac{1}{4}$ lb
Onions: 4
Thyme: 2 oz
Hot Bonny pepper: 1
Powdered clove: $\frac{1}{2}$ teaspoon
Guinea corn flour: $\frac{1}{4}$ lb

Cook all ingredients except guinea corn flour together until peas are tender. Liquid should be reduced to $\frac{1}{3}$ of original volume. Remove the whole pepper and grind the rest in a meat grinder or food processor, retaining the liquid in which cooking was done. Mix guinea corn flour in 1 cup cold water. In a pot of boiling water ($\frac{2}{3}$ pint) add slowly the dissolved guinea corn, stirring all the time. Turn off heat.
Place peas mixture in another pot on the fire, and gradually add cooked guinea corn flour. Keep turning with wooden coo-coo stick. Keep peas mixture stiff – do not add too much liquid. Cook on a very low heat. Simmer for about ten minutes, stirring occasionally.
Jug left over may be kept in refrigerator for days and warmed up when needed. It tends to lose flavour if frozen.

Cattlewash, St Joseph, Barbados   Photography by Willie Alleyne

Steak Margarita

Steaks: 6, about $\frac{1}{2}''$ thick
Salt and black pepper: to taste, or $\frac{1}{4}$
    teaspoon each
Lime juice: 1 tablespoon
Sugar: 1 tablespoon
Cornstarch (St Vincent arrowroot): $\frac{1}{2}$
    teaspoon
Onion: 1 medium, chopped
Sherry: 1 tablespoon
Garlic: 1 clove, crushed
Stock (beef, chicken or pork): 1 tablespoon
Corn oil: 3 tablespoons

Season steaks with salt and black pepper. In a skillet or frying pan, heat oil to moderate temperature. Cook garlic in this oil until burnt or carbonised. Remove garlic and put in steaks in oil, 2 or 3 at a time. Brown steaks approximately 3 minutes on both sides. Remove and place on a platter. Mix lime juice, sherry, sugar and cornstarch in a small bowl. Cook onions until glazed, scraping the bottom of pan to loosen any congealed bits. Add lime mixture and stir until well blended and thick. Pour over steaks and serve hot.

How to Light a Fire

It depends on the kind of fire you wish to light.

If you are using a gas stove, it is much better to strike a match and then turn on the burner you wish to use, bringing the lighted match close to the burner at the time of turning on.

Don't forget that some gas ranges require pressure on the knob controlling the gas before you attempt to twist. If you do not press the knob you may break the bakelite of which most of the knobs are made.

In my Scout Troop they used to tell us you can make fire by rubbing two dry sticks together if you don't happen to have matches.

Cigarette lighters should be used only in extremity. And if you do have a cigarette lighter it is better to light a taper or matchstick with the lighter than to apply the flame of the naked lighter directly to the gas.

In lighting a gas oven it is most important that the match or taper be lit before the gas of the oven is turned on. Failure to observe this rule may result in serious personal injury.

So much for gas.

Electric burners should present no problem, but there are few, if any, recipes which require the controls of electric burners to be kept on 'high' throughout the cooking process. Even in 'stir-fry' cooking, after the pan with oil has been heated to the required temperature the control should be turned down in order to prevent the chemical change which is brought about by the burning of the oil.

We are strongly in favour of the West Indian coal pot, the Japanese habachi and the old wood stove of which the Caledonian is the most celebrated.

Added to these is the 'storebought' barbecue grill, gas-assisted or straight coal burner and the home made barbecue from an oil drum or bricks.

To light a fire in any of these you need: (a) kindling: Use dry twigs broken into lengths of 8″ to 12″, or boxwood of the same length, but splintered into thicknesses of one half to one inch. Twist two or three sheets of newspaper tightly. Place this in the bottom of the coalpot or grill and then criss cross with kindlings, about 12 sticks. Layer these with some larger pieces of firewood of the same length, but up to 2″ thick, and then place about 2 to 3 pounds of coal or brickettes on top. You may sprinkle some kerosene on the grill, half a pint for a large fire.

Strike a match and throw it on the pile of kindling and coal, standing back at least two feet. If you have not sprinkled fuel on the pile you may apply a match directly to the twisted paper which is now under the wood and coal.

It is important that too much coal or brickettes should not smother the fire. It is far better to have a good supply of wood to establish the fire for at least ten minutes before relying exclusively on coal.

If you have bellows you can use them to encourage burning development of the charcoal or brickettes when they have caught. In the old days we used a stiff piece of cardboard or tin, not larger than twelve inches square as a fan, to fan the flames.

The crackling of the burning wood and sparks from the livening coal are memories which those of us who had this chore to perform will remember with nostalgia.

In my pioneering days, I have lit a fire by processing the rays of the sun on paper and kindling through a magnifying glass and also by rubbing dry sticks together.

If you are cooking in the evening the first is impracticable, and if you are hungry or expecting guests to share in your repast, I suggest you forget the second method unless you are out to prove something.

With the Caledonian iron stove, top loading rather than front loading of fuel is suggested in order to get your fire going.

After you have pots (which should be heavy iron ones, preferably) on the two left side burners, then front loading is more practicable in order to keep your fire replenished with either wood or coal.

The beautiful thing about these stoves is their ability to retain an even temperature both on top and in the oven, with a minimum of fuel replenishment.

EWB

Great House, Farley Hill National Park, St Peter, Barbados   Photography by Willie Alleyne

Bacon

Codrington College, St John, Barbados

Photography by Willie Alleyne

Cooking Bacon on top of Stove

Place bacon in cold frying pan. Use low heat. You will learn from experience that bacon is susceptible to rapid chemical change if cooked too quickly. Have you ever noticed the pungent smell of amonia coming from the kitchen while you are getting dressed? Turn the heat low. Save energy. Arrive at work without that smell in your hair.
EWB

Eight Hour Bacon

You need an eye-level oven, preferably electric.
Place strips of bacon on a rack in a shallow pan. Select heat at 125°F, place pan in oven. Go to bed.
When you wake up, turn off oven. Bacon will be ready for your breakfast.

Architectural legacies of Trinidad—The Red House in Abercromby Street, Port of Spain, Trinidad
Courtesy the Trinidad and Tobago Tourist Board

Pork

Baked Pork Chops in a Spicy Tomato Sauce

Pork chops: 6 to 8, loin or other
Salt and freshly ground black pepper:
   1 teaspoon each
Garlic: 1 clove, minced
Cornstarch (St Vincent arrowroot):
   1 teaspoon
Corn oil: 2 tablespoons
Flour: 1 tablespoon
Butter: 1 tablespoon
Tomato paste: 1 teaspoon
Tomato sauce: $\frac{1}{2}$ cup
Water: 1 cup
Red wine: 2 tablespoons
Oregano: 2 teaspoons
Hot sauce: $\frac{1}{2}$ teaspoon
Sugar: 2 teaspoons
Parmesan cheese: 2 tablespoons

Season chops with salt, black pepper, garlic and cornstarch. In a skillet, cook chops in hot oil to brown on both sides. Remove chops on to a baking dish. In a saucepan heat, on a medium-low fire, 1 tablespoon of butter. Mix in the flour until well blended, and cook for a minute until frothing. Add water, wine, tomato sauce and paste, oregano, sugar, salt and hot sauce, stirring constantly for 3 minutes. When well blended, pour over chops. Sprinkle with parmesan cheese and bake for 45 minutes at 325°F. Serve hot.

Braised Pork Hocks in a Tangy Tamarind Sauce

Pork hocks: 6 pieces, $1\frac{1}{2}''$ thick
Soy sauce: 1 tablespoon
Garlic: 1 clove, crushed and minced
Salt: $\frac{1}{2}$ teaspoon or to taste
Black pepper: 1 teaspoon
Sherry: 1 tablespoon
Tamarind sauce (see recipe):
   3 tablespoons
Stock (pork): 1 cup
Water: 1 cup
Corn oil: $\frac{1}{4}$ cup
Cornstarch: 1 teaspoon

Season pork hocks with soy sauce, garlic, salt and pepper. In a large skillet or pot, brown hocks in hot oil. Drain and remove hocks on to a platter. Drain off excess oil from pot and add stock, tamarind sauce, hocks, sherry and water. Cover and cook at low heat for $1\frac{1}{4}$ hours or until hocks become tender. Liquid should be reduced to $\frac{1}{3}$ of volume. Correct flavour of sauce by adding salt if necessary. Thicken sauce with 1 teaspoon cornstarch dissolved in 1 tablespoon of water. Serve hot.

Tamarind Sauce

Tamarind pods: 6
Water: 3 cups
Sugar: 2 tablespoons

Shell pods and remove seeds from pulp. Bring water to boil in a pot. Add pulp and cook at low-medium heat until liquid is reduced to 1 cup in volume. Add sugar and simmer for five minutes.

Strain liquid through a muslin cloth and squeeze as much liquid as possible from the pulp. Store liquid in a covered sterilised jar in the refrigerator if not used immediately.

Braised Pork Hocks in a Tangy Tamarind Sauce
Photography by Willie Alleyne. Styling by Marie Henderson

Garlic Pork

Pork: lean meat of 1 leg, cut into 1″ cubes,
  preferably from male pig not sow
Garlic cloves: 2 to 3 cups, chopped
Thyme leaves (fine): 1 cup
Onions: 4, coarsely chopped
Hot peppers: 2, coarsely chopped
Celery: 1 small bunch, finely chopped
Vinegar: to barely cover pork, etc.
Salt: 1 tablespoon

Quantities of any ingredient may vary to individual taste. More of this or that has little effect on the final product, so the individual can place emphasis where liked. Scald pork cubes in boiling water. Drain and squeeze out water. Sprinkle with salt and leave to drain further. Place vinegar in a large pot and bring to a boil. Boil 5 minutes then set aside to cool. Mix together garlic, thyme, onions, hot pepper and celery.

Containers and covers used for storing meat and seasonings should be thoroughly cleaned, preferably sterilized, and made of glass or plastic (not metal).

In a large container (ware, glass or plastic), place 1 tablespoon salt and meat to quarter fill. Cover with some of the garlic mixture. Add warm vinegar to barely cover.

Continue layering meat, garlic mixture and vinegar until jar is almost full. Seal, or cover tightly.

Stand in a cool place for 7 to 9 days before using. If necessary during this period, tilt jar for a more even distribution of ingredients.

When using, remove meat and a small amount of liquid with a **wooden** spoon. Using an iron pot, fry in a little oil, turning frequently to avoid sticking. Add more oil or spoon off liquid as is necessary. Frying can be a long process and it is advisable not to leave pot unattended.

Meat is cooked when lightly browned on the outside and not pink in the inside when cut.

Midway during frying, a small amount of soy sauce may be added.

Serve hot.

Honey Glazed Spareribs

Spareribs (pork): 5 lbs
Garlic: 2 cloves, crushed and minced
Salt and black pepper: $\frac{1}{2}$ teaspoon each, or
  to taste
Wine vinegar: 2 tablespoons
Tomato ketchup: 3 tablespoons
Worcester sauce: 2 tablespoons
Lime juice: 1 tablespoon
Honey: 3 tablespoons
Onions: $\frac{1}{2}$ cup, chopped
Corn oil: 3 tablespoons
Water: $\frac{1}{2}$ cup

Season spareribs with salt, black pepper and garlic. Heat oil in a pan, and brown onions. Add ketchup, Worcester sauce, honey, lime juice, vinegar and water and cook mixture for 20 minutes at low heat. Grill ribs for 45 minues, basting with the sauce frequently. Remove to platter, cut into plate-size portions and serve hot.

Piquant Pineapple Pork   Photography by Willie Alleyne. Styling by Eleanor Chandler

Piquant Pineapple Pork

Pork: 2 lbs, tenderloin or lean, cut into $\frac{3}{4}''$ pieces
Salt and black pepper: to taste
Sweet peppers: 2 medium, quartered
Pineapple rings: 1 tin, with juice – 10 rings

Batter

Flour: 1 cup
Cornstarch: $\frac{1}{3}$ cup
Egg: 1

Mix ingredients together and add enough water to make a thicky creamy batter.

Sauce

Garlic: 3 cloves, crushed
Ginger: 1 'thumb', crushed
Sugar: $1\frac{1}{2}$ tablespoons
Vinegar: $\frac{1}{4}$ cup
Pineapple juice: $\frac{1}{3}$ cup
Cornstarch: 1 tablespoon, dissolved in 2 tablespoons water

Bring sauce ingredients to a boil and simmer for 10 minutes until well blended. Remove garlic and ginger then add cornstarch mixture to thicken sauce. Remove from heat.

Parsley: 2 sprigs, to garnish
Maraschino cherries: 6, also for garnishing
Corn oil: to deep fry

Season pork with salt and black pepper, dip in batter and deep fry until golden brown, approximately 5 to 10 minutes. Remove from heat and place on serving dish. Quickly fry sweet peppers for 20 seconds, drain off oil and mix with pork. Pour (pineapple) sauce to which 4 quartered pineapple rings have been added, over the pork. Garnish with whole pineapple rings, cherries and parsley, and serve.

Stir-Fry Spicy Pork

Fresh pork: 1 lb, sliced $\frac{1}{4}'' \times 2''$ pieces
Water chestnuts: 1 small can (about 12)
Bamboo shoots (sliced): 1 small can
    ($\frac{1}{2}$ to $\frac{3}{4}$ cup)
Scallions (optional): 4, chopped
Ginger root: 2 teaspoons, chopped
Garlic: 4 cloves, minced
Soy sauce (to marinate pork): 1 tablespoon
Water: 1 tablespoon
Sugar: $\frac{1}{2}$ teaspoon
Cornstarch: 1 tablespoon
Oil: 1 tablespoon
Oil for blanching meat: 3 cups
Soy sauce (seasoning sauce): 1 tablespoon
Vinegar: $\frac{1}{2}$ tablespoon
White wine: $\frac{1}{2}$ tablespoon
Sugar: 1 teaspoon

Salt: $\frac{1}{2}$ teaspoon
Cornstarch: 2 teaspoons
Sesame oil: 1 teaspoon
Black pepper: $\frac{1}{4}$ teaspoon

Add soy sauce, water and sugar to sliced meat, mix thoroughly, add wine and then salt and cornstarch. Mix thoroughly and add 1 tablespoon oil. Mix to keep meat from sticking together. Let stand at least 15 minutes.

Heat oil to 300°F, add pork to blanch till pork changes colour and is cooked. Drain. Pour oil from pan (and save for another use). Re-heat pan with 1 tablespoon oil and add ginger and garlic. Stir-fry a few seconds. Add meat, water chestnuts and bamboo shoots. Stir thoroughly. Add seasoning soy sauce. Sprinkle with scallion mix and serve hot.

Stir-Fry Spicy Pork   Photography by Willie Alleyne. Styling by Jeanine Leemans

Sweet and Sour Spare Ribs

Spare ribs (pork or beef): 2 lbs, cut into
    1″ pieces
Sherry: 2 tablespoons
Cornstarch (St Vincent arrowroot):
    2 tablespoons
Salt and black pepper: to taste or
    $\frac{1}{4}$ teaspoon each
Light soy sauce: 1 tablespoon
Corn oil: $\frac{1}{4}$ cup

Sauce

Sugar: 4 tablespoons
Wine vinegar: 4 tablespoons
Rum (Trinidad or Barbados):
    2 tablespoons
Sesame oil: $\frac{1}{2}$ teaspoon
Light soy sauce: 2 tablespoons
Root ginger: 6 thin slices

Mix sherry, soy sauce, salt and black pepper and cornstarch; season spare ribs and set aside for 1 hour. Heat oil in pan, and brown the spare ribs. Remove the browned spare ribs to a platter.

Drain off excess oil and re-heat pan. Add ginger, and when wilted, add the rest of the sauce ingredients. Bring sauce to a boil and return the spare ribs to the pot. Cook for 3 to 4 minutes, stirring the spare ribs so that they are well coated on all sides. Serve hot.

Stuffed Roast Pork Maraval

Pork: 1 leg, deboned
Garlic: 2 cloves, minced
Light soy sauce: 1 tablespoon
Worcester sauce: 1 tablespoon
Rum (Trinidad or Barbados): 2 oz

Season leg of deboned pork inside and out, with marinade ingredients. Set aside for 2 hours.

Stuffing

Boiled spinach leaves: 2 cups, squeezed
    until pulpy
Breadcrumbs: 1 cup
Wine vinegar: 1 tablespoon
Sugar: 1 tablespoon
Salt and black pepper: to taste, or $\frac{1}{2}$
    teaspoon each
Maraval herbs: thyme, celery, chive: $\frac{1}{2}$
    cup, minced

Mix stuffing ingredients and fill cavity of pork leg, where the bone has been removed. Place stuffed leg in a baking pan; pour 1 cup water in the pan, and roast at 325°F for 25 minutes for each pound of pork. Pork should be well cooked before serving. Slice and serve hot.

Pork and Red Beans

Stewing pork: 1 lb, cut into 1″ pieces
Pickled pigtail: 4 pieces, about 1″ each
Garlic: 1 clove, crushed
Sugar: 1 teaspoon
Red beans: 2 cups, dried
Coconut milk (see recipe): 1 cup
Corn oil: 3 tablespoons

Heat oil in pot. Add garlic and pork to brown. Discard garlic. Add pigtail, red beans, coconut milk and water to cover ingredients. Bring to a boil and simmer for 1 hour or until beans are tender. Serve hot with white rice. Red beans are a very good source of protein in the diet.

Tenderloin Roast Pork

Pork tenderloin: about 2 lbs
Red food colouring: ½ teaspoon
Sherry: 2 tablespoons
Chinese hoisin sauce: 1½ tablespoons
Salt: ½ teaspoon
Honey or sugar: 2 teaspoons
Corn oil: 1 tablespoon

In a bowl, mix all ingredients into a paste. Season pork fillets with mixture and let it marinate for 2 to 3 hours. Pork fillets are long strips of meat, approximately 8″ by 2″, so they can be cooked more quickly than thicker pieces of meat, and at a higher temperature. The higher heat causes the marinade to become veneered on to the meat and gives a reddish, honeyed colour on the surface, so that when sliced crosswise, the characteristic reddish brown edge of the slices is seen vividly.

There should be 2 wire racks in the oven, set at different levels. The pork fillets rest on the upper rack, and a wide pan or dish is placed on the lower rack to collect the drippings while roasting. Set temperature at 400°F. Roast for 30 minutes, turning pork halfway. Remove from oven, slice crosswise, and serve.

Treasure Rolls Filling

Mung bean noodles (fun see): 2 cups, soaked and strained
Light soy sauce: 2 tablespoons
Pork: 1 lb, minced
Shrimps: $\frac{1}{2}$ lb, deveined and minced
Bamboo shoots: $\frac{1}{2}$ cup, shredded
Chinese mushrooms: $\frac{1}{2}$ cup, soaked, drained and chopped
Scallions or chive: 2 blades, minced
Sherry: 1 tablespoon
Sugar: 1 tablespoon
Sesame oil: 1 teaspoon

Soak noodles (*fun see*) until soft and transparent. Drain and set aside.
Mix all ingredients together. Add more soy for taste if necessary.

Thai rice wrappers (rice paper skins): 10 round, approximately 9″ diameter
Corn oil: 3 to 4 cups

Lay one wrapper on a flat surface. Dampen the skin lightly with warm water until it softens.
Place filling at one end of wrapper and fold into a roll. Tuck ends under roll. Repeat until all have been rolled.
Heat oil in a pot large enough to hold stuffed rolls. When moderately hot, put one or two rolls in pot and cook until crispy – about 5 to 7 minutes.
Remove to a dish and drain on paper towels. Continue until all are cooked.
Cut into 2 to 3 sections each, and serve, preferably hot.

Treasure Rolls

Photography by Willie Alleyne. Styling by Jeanine Leemans

Carnival in Trinidad

Courtesy Roger Cambridge

West Indian Rice Recipes

West Indian Rice Recipes

There is no food cooked with more imprecision than rice. Boiling rice can produce consistent results if you use a simple formula:

Two cups uncooked rice can serve four persons.

Place $1\frac{1}{2}$ cups of water for each cup of rice in a pot. Three cups of water for 2 cups rice, 6 cups water for 4 cups or 2 pints rice.

Bring water to boil. Add rice, 1 teaspoon salt, 1 small onion, 1 hot pepper, 2 cloves garlic and 1 tablespoon butter, margarine or cooking oil. Turn heat down immediately so that water is just bubbling, but not vigorously. Cover pot and check grains for tenderness in 25 to 30 minutes. Remove from heat, and leave covered for another 20 minutes. Dish up when ready to serve.

Rice may be cooked with chopped spinach, chopped white cabbage, green chopped cabbage leaves. It is not necessary to use more water.

When cooking rice with peas, i.e. green peas, dry peas, lentils, red beans, etc, the peas or beans should be boiled first in two to three cups of water to each cup of peas/beans. Add 4 ounces of salt meat or pigtail and cook at the same time with thyme, hot pepper and 2 quartered onions. When the peas are tender, liquid should be poured off to ensure that you have 2 cups of liquid for each cup of rice. Pour rice in pot with peas and add back liquid to ensure that there are 2 cups liquid per cup of rice. If necessary, add boiling water. Cover pot.

Lower heat to simmer as before for 20 minutes or until liquid is fully absorbed.

Red beans tend to take longer than green peas or lentils. Coconut milk (see preparation) adds a delicate flavour to peas and rice or red beans and rice. Jamaicans tend to do this better than their opposite numbers in the Eastern Caribbean.

EWB

To Boil Plain Rice so that it is Grainy

Measure rice in cups.

Wash and clean rice thoroughly. Drain off water as much as possible. For each cup of rice (which has been drained of excess water that was used in washing it), add:

1 cup of water.

Rice should be in a covered pot and put on medium heat on stove until the water boils off – this is usually in about 10 minutes if about 3 cups of rice are being cooked.

When there is no more water visible on the top of the rice, turn the heat down to the lowest mark (so that a very low heat is used) and leave the rice to steam for about $\frac{1}{2}$ hour at this very low heat.

DO NOT UNCOVER POT while rice is steaming at this very low temperature.

Rice cooked by this method comes out grainy and the bottom will not be burnt.
AVE LEE

Cooking Rice in Bed

Boil water as before and add to rice and other ingredients. Use a pot with a tight fitting cover. Try a small pressure cooker if your covers do not fit tightly.

Remove pot from heat. Wrap in a full edition of your local newspaper – *New York Times*, *Montreal Star* or *Miami Herald* are too bulky. Then wrap in a blanket. Place between sheets and bedspread at the bottom of your bed.

Go to the theatre or get on with your other cooking. In about 2 hours your rice will be cooked. Guaranteed not to burn, no matter how long you leave it!

This formula was discovered in London when we had one of our frequent power failures years ago. Power or no power, it became my standard method of preparation. Save energy!
EWB

Caribbean Fried Rice

Boiled rice: 6–8 cups (see method of boiling rice)
Bacon: 3 slices, chopped
Onions: $\frac{1}{2}$ cup, minced
Chive or scallions: 3 tablespoons, chopped
Sweet peppers: $\frac{1}{2}$ cup, chopped
Celery: 2 tablespoons, chopped
Carrots: $\frac{1}{2}$ cup, diced
Cauliflower: $\frac{1}{2}$ cup, chopped
Tenderloin pork or shrimp: $\frac{1}{2}$ lb, diced
Sugar: 2 teaspoons
Butter: 2 oz
Garlic: 1 teaspoon, minced finely

Oil (corn or similar): 1 tablespoon
Salt and pepper: to taste

Dice pork (or shrimp). Season with garlic, salt and pepper and 1 tablespoon of the chive.

Rice must be freshly boiled and grainy.

Heat 1 tablespoon oil in large pot (preferably iron). Add bacon then pork (or shrimp). Stir fry for 2 minutes on hot fire until cooked. Add chive and onions. Stir for a few seconds, then put the vegetables in and stir for $\frac{1}{2}$ minute. Add butter at this stage, turning down the heat so that butter will not burn. Add rice, stir until well mixed, adding salt and pepper. Remove from fire and transfer to serving dish. Sprinkle chopped chive on top and serve hot.

Chicken with Tarragon Sauce. Caribbean Fried Rice. Calypso 'Birds'
Photography by Willie Alleyne. Styling by Marie Henderson

Privilege

Signal Tower, St George, Barbados

Photography Willie Alleyne

Privilege

We agreed to call our book *Privilege* because 1) it is unusual; 2) it is the name of one of the Barbadian dishes frequently cooked in agricultural areas; 3) it is simple to prepare and 4) it is unique.

Although I had eaten this dish on visits to rural homes, I did not fully appreciate its complete nutritional value and simplicity until I asked for the recipe some thirty years ago. This is the complete, one pot meal. You need:

Rice: 3 cups
Ochroes (okras): 6
Hot pepper: 1
Pigtail or salt beef: 1 pigtail or 4 oz saltbeef
Garlic: 2 cloves
Salted codfish or salt fish: 8 oz
Onions: 3 medium
Margarine or butter: 2 tablespoons or *cooking oil:* $\frac{1}{2}$ cup

First, cut your saltbeef or pigtail into pieces about $1\frac{1}{2}''$. Place in 3 pints of cold water in small pan. Bring to boil and simmer for 15 minutes, remove from heat, throw away the water. Boil codfish for a similar period and throw water away. Purpose is to remove excess salt. Remove bones if any. Peel onions and cut into segments, not circular rings. Make sure okras are not stringy when you buy them. The tips should snap off easily. Cut off large ends by the stem. Cut each okra crosswise in two or four pieces.

Place oil or margarine in a large pot, capacity at least 6 pints. Heat oil and throw in onions and 2 pieces of peeled garlic. At the same time, bring a pot of 6 cups water to the boil. Pour boiling water into the pot with onions. Put okras and salt meat into boiling water. Cook for 15 or 20 minutes in tightly covered pot, low heat, just boiling. Put in your rice, pepper and chunks of fish – do not shred. Cover pot and leave on low simmering heat for 15 to 20 minutes. Remove and serve or leave in pot until ready.

You may use more okras and more onion too, if you like. That is your privilege. Serves six, (or four hungry people).
EWB

Interior of Gasparee Caves, Gasparee Island, off Trinidad
Courtesy the Trinidad and Tobago Tourist Board.

West Indian Recipes

Breadfruit

If you don't know what it is, then buy one. It is about the size of a small football – about 6 inches in diameter – or it may be elongated about 7 to 8 inches long and 5 inches in diameter.

Make sure it is firm and even hard. Cut the breadfruit in quarters lengthwise through the stem. Peel off the green outer skin with a knife. Remove also the porous core of the fruit. Place segments in a saucepan, cover with cold water with a level teaspoon of salt, and bring to the boil. Turn heat down to simmer and when a fork can penetrate without much pressure being used, remove from heat and pour off water.

Breadfruit may be served:

1. as a vegetable in this state or
2. it may be mashed with a tablespoon of butter or margarine and a little milk, like mashed potatoes
3. a further refinement is breadfruit coo-coo, when it is boiled a little longer until very soft and put in a blender or food processor with an onion or two, and finely chopped saltbeef (2 or 3 ounces). Put back in pan and stir with a flat wooden stick for a few minutes, adding butter or margarine to taste. A ripe breadfruit is better for this. However, if
4. you wish to make breadfruit chips or fried breadfruit slices, a greener fruit is better, and it should not be boiled too long. It should be a bit undercooked and very firm when removed from the water.
5. Breadfruit also makes a popular soup. Prepare as before. Place half a breadfruit in 3 pints water with 4 ounces salt beef or pigtail. Boil until soft. Add 1 large chopped onion and some thyme and small piece of fresh hot pepper. Use ricer to mash fruit in pot. Add 1 pint milk, simmer for a few minutes over a low fire and serve. Sprinkle some chopped parsley in each bowl after laying out.
6. Pickled breadfruit is made by cutting the boiled fruit in chunks, like in potato salad, then placing in a pickle as for soused pork. (see *Souse* recipe)

Add some flakes of boiled salt cod fish for a complete dish on its own.

Bul Jol

Cucumber: 1
Salt fish: $\frac{1}{2}$ lb
Avocado: $\frac{1}{2}$
Tomatoes: 2, ripe but firm
Onions: 2 medium, peeled
Lime: $\frac{1}{2}$
Hot pepper: $\frac{1}{2}$, red
Coconut jelly, medium hard: from 2 coconuts

Soak salt fish overnight in cold water, or for two hours, according to quality. Less salt, less soaking. Remove from water and shred, or rather, flake. Good quality cod flakes well.

Rub a pyrex bowl well with the pepper (using a wooden spoon) and remove. Peel cucumber with knife or a potato peeler. Place fish in bowl. Slice cucumber thinly. Slice firm tomatoes thinly. Slice onions cross wise in their rings. Stir fish for $\frac{1}{2}$ minute or so in bowl. Layer in cucumbers, onions and tomatoes. Cut the medium hard coconut jelly into small bits and add. Squeeze $\frac{1}{2}$ lime overall. Serve when ready with crackers or toast (a cold dish).

Bul Jol   Photography by Willie Alleyne. Styling by Marie Henderson

Coo-Coo (Barbadian)

In the Leeward and Virgin Islands *Coo-Coo* is made without ochroes, and is known as *Fengi*.

Ochroes (okras): 6
Corn meal (maize): 1 cup
Cold water: 3 cups
Butter or margarine: 1 tablespoon
Salt: 1 teaspoon

1. Place corn meal in a bowl and pour 1 cup of cold water over it. This is called 'wetting'. In some islands, the corn meal is poured directly into the boiling okra stock.
2. Wash and cut ochroes across, discarding tips and stems. Place in 2 cups boiling water with salt, and cook for about 5 minutes. Pour off half water, and set aside.
3. Add wetted meal to ochro mixture gradually, stirring with flat wooden stick (coo-coo stick) to ensure there are no lumps.
After all the meal has been added, keep heat low and add some of the ochro water which you set aside at stage 2.
Keep stirring until smooth and meal is thoroughly cooked and stiff. Add butter. Turn off heat and serve when ready with boiled fish or beef stew or curry. Boiled sweet potato is also a great compliment. Best when served hot.

A coo-coo stick is shaped like a miniature cricket bat. It is about 14″ long, made from wood, and is obtainable in Barbados.

Mettagee (Guyana)

In almost all the West Indian Islands, variations of this dish are known by different names. In Jamaica, it is 'Run Down', in Trinidad, Grenada and St Vincent it is 'Oil Down', as it is (b)oiled down in the preparation.

Salted meat – pigtail or salt beef: 1 lb
Salt fish: 1 lb
Onions: 4 large or 6 medium
Ochroes (okras): 6
Breadfruit: 1 medium size, hard
Yam or sweet potatoes: 1 lb
Plantains: 2, ripe but firm
Coconut milk (see recipe): 1 pint
Hot peppers: 2, whole
Thyme: to taste, or 1 teaspoon

1. Boil salted meat for about 45 minutes in water.
2. Soak salt fish in cold water for about 2 hours. Pour off water.
3. Peel breadfruit, yam and onions, and cut up.
4. Cut plantains in half and remove skin. Place coconut milk in pot.
Put breadfruit, yams (or sweet potatoes), salt meat, peppers and thyme in the pot and cover tightly. Cook until soft.
5. When the 'provisions' are almost tender, put in the plantains, ochroes, onions and salt fish on top.
6. Simmer slowly for 15 minutes.
Remove from heat and serve with spinners (dumplings) if desired. The 'provisions' can be cut up into smaller pieces, and the salt fish flaked before serving.

(B)oil Down

This dish is popular in many of the islands of the West Indies. There are different versions, where other ground provisions, as cassava, eddoes, etc or green plantain, or dumplings, are included or used instead of breadfruit. In Guyana, it is known as 'Mettagee'. This recipe comes from Grenada. In Jamaica, it is called 'Run Down'.

Breadfruit: 1, medium sized
Pigtail or salt meat: $\frac{1}{2}$ lb, cut into 2″ pieces
Hot pepper (green): 1, left whole
Onion: 1, small, chopped
Chive or scallion: 1 bunch, chopped
Garlic: 2 cloves, chopped
Chadon bené: 1 leaf, chopped finely
Coconut milk: 2 cups (see recipe)

Boil the pigtail or salt meat in water until soft. Throw off this water, and add 1 cup more water. Peel and slice the breadfruit into long slices of about $1\frac{1}{2}″$ at the middle part of each slice. Add the breadfruit to the salt meat, the coconut milk, chive, chadon bené, garlic and hot pepper. Add salt if desired. Let boil slowly until liquid has 'boiled down'. Make sure not to let the hot pepper burst. Serve hot. Delicious also when cold.

Red Beans

Red or kidney beans: 1 package (12 to 16 oz)
Salt beef or pigtail: $\frac{1}{4}$ lb
Sugar: 2 tablespoons
Hot pepper: 1, leave whole
Onion: 2 medium
Coconut milk (see recipe): 1 pint

Boil meat. Throw off water. Pour 2 pints fresh water in pot. Put in beans and cook until they are tender. Pour off excess liquid, leaving just enough to cover beans. Add 1 pint coconut milk. Add pepper and cut up onions.
Cover and simmer slowly, taking care not to let the hot pepper burst. Add spinners (see recipe) just before serving.

Red beans may be served as a separate dish or with salt mackerel which has been gently boiled and buttered, removing bones after boiling.

Pepper Pot

In the southern Caribbean, pepperpot is not a soup, but a substantial meat dish of which the basic secret is the preservative quality of the cassava plant utilised in the preparation of cassareep. The Amerindian tribes of the Guyanas who inhabited the Amazon, Orinoco and Essequibo river basins of South America, hunters in their stage of development, would cook their game whether meat or fowl, in large clay cauldrons which were kept simmering over open fires by the tribes, and replenished from time to time, as the hunters returned from the chase. Cassareep not only preserved the meat, but added a delicate flavour to the cooking. The best cassareep is made in Guyana, although the ingredients are available all over the Caribbean. We have included a recipe for making cassareep in case you cannot find it in your local supply store.

Accessories

Cheese cloth or gauze: 1 piece, 8″ square
Large clay pot with cover or a Dutch oven is a reasonable substitute
A deep cast-iron skillet or a deep pot
A very large mixing bowl or pyrex bowl

Cassareep (see recipe): 1 cup
Stewing beef: 1 lb, good quality
Lean pork (optional): ½ lb
Cow heel or pig's trotters: 1 cow heel, or 4 pig's trotters, either of which should be well cleaned and cut up into 2″ sections
Oxtail: 1, well cleaned with skin on and cut up by your butcher. If only skinned oxtail is available, buy two one-pound packages
Hot peppers (left whole): 4, fresh, stems removed
Thyme: 2 oz
Garlic: 4 cloves
Salt: 2 teaspoons
Brown sugar: 2 oz
Cooking oil: 4 oz
Salt beef: 6 chunks, 2″

Cut beef, pork and salt beef into chunks about 2″ square. Wash all meat, including oxtail, trotters (or cow heel) in cleaned stainless steel sink, or large pan or plastic bowl. Dry beef and pork thoroughly. Drain other washed meat.

Heat ½ cup of oil in iron skillet. Quickly sear beef and oxtail. Remove and place in mixing bowl or pyrex bowl. Cover with clean cloth or kitchen towel.

Mix 4 cups of cold water with 1 cup cassareep. Add salt. Place trotters and/or cut-up cow heel in clay pot and pour diluted cassareep over this to cover. Add salt beef and oxtail. Wash peppers, thyme and garlic, and place on gauze or cheese cloth. Make a bag by bringing your corners together, and tying with strong length of twine that is doubled. Leave both ends of twine about 12 inches long, to hang over edge of pot, or to tie to the lid for removing bag of peppers, etc from pot.

Cook slowly for about 1½ hours. Add beef and pork and pepper bag. Cook slowly for another hour or until all meat is tender, but not dissolved. Add sugar. Simmer 15 minutes. Heat and serve when ready, leaving balance in clay pot, which should be heated up each day for 15 minutes before eating.

If it is intended to keep the *Pepper Pot* for any length of time, we recommend that it be placed in containers and frozen. Remove from freezer and thaw to room temperature when needed. Heat to boiling for about 15 minutes before serving. End of *Pepper Pot*.
EWB

Pepper Pot

Photography by Willie Alleyne. Styling by Marie Henderson

Cassareep

Cassava: 4 lbs, peeled
Brown sugar: 1 tablespoon (heaping)
Cinnamon powder: 1 teaspoon
Cloves (ground): $\frac{1}{2}$ teaspoon
Water: $\frac{1}{2}$ pint

Wash the peeled cassava thoroughly under running water, dry with paper towels. Grate finely on grater or in electric blender (cut up before putting in electric appliance). Remove to a bowl and add cold water to the grated mixture, stirring well. Squeeze the liquid through a wet muslin cloth, twisting the cloth to extract as much liquid as you can. Set aside the grated cassava for possible future use. Put the squeezed cassava liquid into a pan, add cinnamon, cloves and brown sugar and bring to a boil. Lower the heat and let the mixture simmer slowly, stirring occasionally, until it is thick and syrup-like.
If a darker mixture is desired, burnt sugar or browning liquid can be added to darken the cassareep. Makes about $\frac{1}{2}$ pint and is used in making *Pepper Pot*. Can be stored in a cool place in the kitchen, or in the refrigerator. A clean bottle with a tight cork or stopper should be used and, of course, label the bottle, and put the date made.

Pudding

Sweet potatoes: 2–3 lbs, peeled and grated
Onions: 3 medium/large, finely chopped
Chive or spring onions: 6 oz, finely chopped
Thyme leaves: 2 oz, shredded
Salt: 2 teaspoons
Hot pepper: 1
Clove: 1 level teaspoon, powdered
Black pepper: 1 teaspoon
Vinegar: 2 tablespoons, brown
Pig's belly (casing): 3 feet, approximately 1″ × 1″ diameter
Pork stock: $1\frac{1}{2}$ pints approx.

Pudding and souse is a Barbadian dish, the pudding part of which calls for a lot of preparation, such as grating of sweet potatoes, chopping seasonings, stuffing casing, usually thoroughly washed pig's belly, careful cooking to minimise bursting, and so on.
People who sell this delicacy wake up very early on Saturday mornings, at four or five o'clock, to be ready to sell by ten or eleven – not recommended for busy or impatient bachelors!
I have developed a mechanical approach to what would otherwise be a laborious chore.
You need a heavy Kenwood Chef. Peel two or three pounds of ordinary sweet potatoes – not the American yam variety or yellow caroline leaf type. Cut potatoes into 2″ to 3″ sections and grate in machine with grating attachment.
Take 3 medium to large onions; 6 ounces of chive or spring onions; chop finely with 2 ounces of shredded thyme leaves, 2 teaspoons salt, 1 hot burning pepper. Chop with Chinese chopper. Add 1 level tea-

View from St John's Church, St John, Barbados   Photography by Willie Alleyne

spoon powdered clove, 1 teaspoon black pepper, 2 tablespoons brown vinegar. Blend all in large bowl with grated potatoes. If you have a food processor, pass the mixture through the machine using the metal meat blade until a fine paste results. This makes cooking quicker and easier. If you don't own a food processor you can use the potato grated by the Kenwood or a hand grater. It takes longer – the only difference. Thoroughly wash with lime and salt and rinse under running water about 3 feet of medium-size – 1″ to $1\frac{1}{2}$″ diameter – pig's belly (casing). Tie one end with strong cord.

Add 1 to $1\frac{1}{2}$ pints of cold stock left from boiling pork to the potato mixture. Use a funnel, metal or plastic with an opening at least $\frac{1}{2}$″ to $\frac{3}{4}$″. Take open end of casing and slide over the funnel holding firmly with one hand. Transfer mixture with a ladle into the funnel. Here you will need some assistance because someone will have to concentrate on holding the funnel and casing over a large bowl. Push mixture through funnel with round handle of wooden spoon. At intervals of 12 inches, tie off casing with strong twine or white cord. Do not use thread or fine twine which will cut through casing. Tie about three inches above level of mixture to allow for expansion of potato. Continue process until mixture is used up. Tie off top as before.

Place a large pot on fire half filled with water. Put pudding in pot. Bring pot to boil and turn immediately on low heat to simmer gently. Pudding is cooked only when mixture does not ooze through skin when stuck with a toothpick – thirty-five to forty minutes.

The fully mechanised procedure is to utilise the Kenwood sausage stuffing attachment instead of a funnel and tie in same manner at intervals.

Souse

Pig's head and/or *Trotters* and/or *Any choice cut of pork* and/or *Ox tongue:*
2 lbs
Salt: 1 tablespoon

Pudding goes with souse like bacon goes with eggs.

Probably because of the amount of work involved, pudding and souse are usually eaten on Saturdays in Barbados. Souse may be done any day in the week because it is a lot easier to prepare. Traditionally made from pig's head and trotters, there is no reason why souse should not be made from choice cuts of pork and for those who have to avoid pork for dietary reasons, ox tongue is excellent in pickle. Or for a family party, use all three – pork, trotters and tongue.

If you do wish to use the pig's head, have your butcher cut it into four or eight pieces. Slit trotters in half. Use the amount of pork you require. Flap loin or whatever. Place in large pot of water, add a tablespoon of salt and boil until tender. Remove from heat and plunge into cold water. Leave in water until ready with pickle.
EWB

Pickle

Pickle is for souse. Pickle is for breadfruit. Pickle is for breadfruit and salted cod.

Onions: 3, medium to large
Hot pepper: 1, large red
Cucumbers: 2
Limes: 2 juicy
Salt: 2 teaspoons
Sweet pepper: 1 green

Peel onions and cucumbers. Wash and chop hot and sweet peppers in $\frac{1}{4}''$ chunks. Chop onions and cucumbers into same size pieces as peppers. Place in a large glass or ware mixing bowl and add salt to taste. Stir all ingredients together. More cucumber may be used if desired. Leave to settle for one hour or more in refrigerator. Remove pork from water. Peel layers of skin off tongue if being used. Cut meat in pieces $1\frac{1}{2}''$ long × $\frac{1}{2}''$ thick. Leave trotters as they are. Throw all into pickle. Leave for $\frac{1}{2}$ hour at least before serving.
EWB

Spinners or Dumplings

(for *Pea Soup* or *Beef Soup*)

Flour: 2 cups
Baking powder: 1 tablespoon
Salt: 1 level teaspoon
Sugar: 2 level teaspoons
Cold water: 1 cup

Sift flour, baking powder and salt together into a medium-size mixing bowl. Dissolve sugar in cup of cold water. Add liquid to flour, etc in bowl and blend into a stiff dough. Wash and dry your hands. Remove mixture from bowl, and knead for a minute or two on a board, adding a little flour if necessary to ensure that the dough is not sticky. Divide dough into three equal portions, and roll each on board into rolls, not more than $\frac{1}{2}''$ in diameter. With a sharp knife, cut each roll diagonally into pieces about $\frac{1}{4}''$ in thickness. Drop the 'spinners' into soup and cook for fifteen minutes.

Vegetables: Melongene, Sweet Pepper, Carailli, Ginger, Christophene, White Radish, Carrots, Tomato, Ochroes
Photography by Willie Alleyne. Styling by Marie Henderson

Vegetables

Christophene and Cheese

Christophenes (chayotes): 4, green, about
  4″ long
Cheese (Cheddar): 6 ounces, grated or cut
  up
Raisins: a handful

Slice christophenes in half, lengthwise, and boil in skins until just soft. Scoop out centre core with a teaspoon. Melt grated cheese with raisins in a pan. When the cheese is melted, fill the centres of the christophene halves with this cheese mixture, using a teaspoon. Decorate top of cheese with raisins. Serve hot.

Christophene and Cheese   Photography by Willie Alleyne. Styling by Marie Henderson

Melongene en Pirogue with Topping of Seafood Stuffing

Melongene (aubergine, eggplant or balangan): 2 or 3, medium-size
Fish: King, Carite or similar – 2 fillets (4–6 oz)
Shrimp: 8 medium-size, shelled and deveined
Chive: ½ cup, chopped
Garlic: 1 teaspoon, minced
Vinegar: 1 tcaspoon
Salt: 1 teaspoon
Thyme: 1 teaspoon
Cornstarch: 1 teaspoon
Breadcrumbs: 1 tablespoon
Parmesan cheese: 2 tablespoons

Season fish slices with garlic, salt and pepper. Dust with flour and fry in hot oil until cooked (3–5 minutes).
Transfer to a plate. When cool, remove the skin and mash fish with a spoon or fork. Do the same with the uncooked shrimp until blended. Add the uncooked seasoning ingredients including the cornstarch and breadcrumbs into the fish-shrimp mixture until well blended, adding salt and pepper to taste.
Cut melongenes lengthwise ½″ thick. You should have about 6 oval (boat shaped) slices. Put into boiling water for 2–3 minutes. Remove and dry with paper towels

Batter

Eggs: 2
Flour: 1 tablespoon
Butter (melted): 1 tablespoon
Salt and pepper: to taste

Beat eggs, add melted butter, salt and pepper then sprinkle flour into mixture and blend. Dip the melongene slices in batter on both sides. Put in baking dish. Pour the seafood mixture on top of the melogene slices. Sprinkle with breadcrumbs and parmesan cheese and bake in oven at 375°F for about 25 minutes. Serve hot.

Plantain Pinwheels

Ripe plantains: 4, peeled
Shrimp, medium: 16, shelled and
   de-veined
Chive or scallions: 2 tablespoons, chopped
Sherry: 2 teaspoons
Sesame oil: 1 teaspoon
Light soy sauce: 1 teaspoon
Cornstarch (St Vincent arrowroot):
   1 teaspoon
Cayenne pepper: a dash
Salt: $\frac{1}{4}$ teaspoon

Cut plantains lengthwise into long slices $\frac{1}{8}''$ thick. Discard the 2 rounded end slices. Mince the shrimp into a paste and add other ingredients. Roll the long plantain slices into wheel shapes and hold together with toothpicks. Fill the 'wheels' on both sides of the toothpicks with the shrimp paste. Put on a greased baking pan. Sprinkle top with cayenne pepper and brush with oil. Bake at 375°F for 15 minutes, or until cooked. Serve hot.

Plantain Pirogues

Ripe plantains: 4, peeled
Bacon: 4 strips, chopped
Cornstarch (St Vincent arrowroot):
   1 teaspoon
Breadcrumbs: 4 tablespoons
Cheddar cheese, grated: 4 tablespoons
Cinnamon powder: 1 teaspoon
Bitters (Angostura): 1 teaspoon

Cut plantains lengthwise into halves. Scoop out the inner centre portions of each plantain half. Brush centres with oil. Purée or mash the scooped out plantain to a pulpy mixture, then add the rest of the ingredients except the cinammon. Fill the hollowed out centre of the plantain with this mixture, making the filling rounded. Sprinkle top with the cinnamon powder. Bake at 400°F for 15 minutes and serve hot.

Plantain Pinwheels and Plantain Pirogues
Photography by Willie Alleyne. Styling by Marie Henderson

Pumpkin Fritters   Photography by Willie Alleyne. Styling by Jeanine Leemans

Pumpkin Fritters

Fresh pumpkin: 1 lb
Eggs: 2
Sugar: 4 tablespoons
Flour: 5 tablespoons
Butter or margarine: 1 tablespoon
Cooking oil: $\frac{1}{2}$ cup

Peel off skin of pumpkin. Cut in pieces about 2 inches square or similar.
Place pieces in pot with water to cover, and cook until tender. Remove from fire. Pour off water. Crush cooked pumpkin in a mixing bowl. Add sugar. Stir. Add butter. Stir. Add eggs. Stir. Add flour slowly and keep stirring.

Heat oil in shallow skillet or frying pan. Drop one spoonful of mixture at a time into hot oil until pan is comfortably full. Turn fritters over to fry on other side, and remove when golden brown in colour.

Spinach Cakes Photography by Willie Alleyne. Styling by Jeanine Leemans

Spinach Cakes

Spinach: 8 oz
Egg: 1
White pepper: $\frac{1}{2}$ teaspoon
Butter: 2 tablespoons, melted
Fresh milk: $\frac{1}{2}$ cup
Onions: 1 tablespoon, chopped
Salt: $\frac{1}{2}$ teaspoon
Breadcrumbs: $\frac{1}{2}$ cup
Flour: $\frac{1}{2}$ cup
Baking powder: $\frac{1}{2}$ teaspoon

Wash spinach leaves after removing stems, and chop finely. Beat egg in a mixing bowl. Add onion, melted butter and spinach. Sift in flour, breadcrumbs, salt and baking powder, and blend well. Add some milk to make mixture just firm enough to drop from a spoon. Heat oil for deep frying in a suitable skillet or frying pan. Drop mixture in hot fat by the spoonful, and cook until golden.

Steamed Bitter Melon (Carailli) with Fish Stuffing
Photography by Willie Alleyne. Styling by Marie Henderson

Steamed Bitter Melon (Carailli) with Fish Stuffing

Bitter melon (carailli): 3, green ones
Glutinous fish mixture (see recipe): 1½ cups
Thyme: 2 teaspoons, chopped

Cut bitter melons (carailli) into 2 or 3 inch portions, remove the centre portion with the seeds, leaving cylindrical shaped sections of the carailli.
Boil in salted water for 1½ minutes, remove from water and dry. Blend thyme with fish mixture.
Stuff each portion of carailli with the fish mixture.
Place on dish and steam in a steamer for ½ hour, until cooked.
Serve on a dish, hot.

Note   Shrimp may be substituted for fish in the glutinous fish mixture.

Stuffed Sweet Peppers

Sweetpeppers (Bell peppers): 8 large, halved and seeded
Pork, beef or shrimp: 1 lb, minced
Chive or scallion: 2 blades, chopped
Light soy sauce: 2 tablespoons
Sherry: 2 tablespoons
Celery: 1 tablespoon, minced
Salt and black pepper: to taste, or ½ teaspoon each
Cornstarch (St Vincent arrowroot): 2 tablespoons
Sesame oil: 1 teaspoon
Garlic: 1 clove, minced
Sugar: 4 teaspoons
Corn oil: 4 tablespoons

Mix together chive, sherry, 1 tablespoon soy sauce, salt and pepper, meat (or shrimp), 2 teaspoons sugar, garlic, celery and cornstarch. Stuff the pepper halves with mixture. Heat oil in pan, and place the stuffed peppers, meat side down, in the pan and cook until stuffing is browned. Transfer to a baking dish, with the stuffing side on top. Mix the remaining soy sauce, sugar and sesame oil and sprinkle over the stuffed peppers. Bake in oven at 325°F for 25 minutes. Serve hot.

Vegetables—Bodi, Green Beans, Cauliflower, Cabbage, Root Ginger, White Pumpkin
Photography by Willie Alleyne. Styling by Marie Henderson

Soups

Cow Heel Soup

Cow heel: 2 lbs, (1″ slices)
Pumpkin: ¼ lb
Carrot: ½ lb
Eddoes (or tannias or similar): ½ lb
Onion: 1 small, chopped
Chive and thyme: 1 tablespoon, chopped
Garlic: 3 cloves
Salt: ½ teaspoon or to taste
Dumplings (see recipe): about 12

Wash and clean cow heel and pressure cook in water for half hour (or boil in water until gristle is soft) with onion, chive and garlic. Boil and peel carrots and cut in round slices, boil and peel eddoes and cut in halves, peel pumpkin and cut into 1″ cubes. Make dumplings and add with all the peeled ingredients to the pot. Add water (to make about 4 cups liquid) and salt and bring mixture to a boil. Lower heat and cook for about 30 minutes or until everything is tender and soft. Serve hot.

This soup is very popular in Trinidad and is believed to be nourishing besides being very tasty.

Callaloo and Crab

Dasheen leaves or callaloo bush: 1 bunch
Ochroes: 12
Crabs: 2 medium or 3 small
Pigtail: 1
Ham bone: optional
Chive or scallions: 1 bunch, chopped
Onion: 2 medium, chopped
Fine thyme: 2 sprigs, chopped
Hot pepper: 1, green
Garlic: 1 clove, chopped
Seasoning peppers: 2, optional
Celery leaves: optional, a small piece, chopped

Strip stalks and midribs from dasheen leaves, wash and cut into fine pieces. Clean crabs. Wash and cut up ochroes and seasonings. In a pot, put crabs and pigtail first, then sprinkle chopped seasonings (chive, onion, garlic, thyme, celery leaves and chopped seasoning peppers without the seeds) over them, then add chopped ochroes, dasheen leaves and stalks with whole hot pepper. Pour 2 to 3 cups of boiling water into pot, and cook to boiling point.
Simmer until everything is soft (about an hour).
Swizzle thoroughly until well blended. One tablespoon of butter may be added and some black pepper. Hot pepper should not be allowed to burst, and should be taken out of the callaloo before swizzling is done.
Chicken stock may be added instead of the water. The pigtail should be soaked first before cooking, so that it would not be too salt and it should be cut into pieces. A ham bone would add to the flavour. Serve hot, either as a soup or over rice.

Callaloo and Crab Soup

Photography by Willie Alleyne. Styling by Marie Henderson

Peanut Butter Soup

Chicken: 1 whole, 3 lbs
Peanut butter: 4 tablespoons
Tomato paste: 4 tablespoons
Tomatoes (fresh): 4 ripe, large
Onions: 2 large
Paprika: 1 teaspoon
Nutmeg: $\frac{1}{4}$ teaspoon
Salt: $\frac{1}{2}$ teaspoon
Bay leaves: 3
Tarragon: $\frac{1}{4}$ teaspoon
Bouillon cubes: 2 (chicken flavoured)
Corn oil: 1 tablespoon

Clean and joint chicken into serving-size pieces. Season with paprika, salt and tarragon. Let stand for $\frac{1}{2}$ hour.
Boil onions and fresh tomatoes for about 5 minutes in 8 cups water. Strain off water into a large bowl to be used later. Purée onions and tomatoes in blender (if you have one). Heat 1 tablespoon corn oil in a large saucepan, and pour in the pureé of onions and tomatoes. Add tomato paste, peanut butter, bouillon cubes and water from onions and tomatoes and stir mixture until well blended (five minutes) Add chicken, keep stirring. Cook for at least 30 minutes until chicken is cooked. Remove from heat and serve hot.

Quick Soups

Stock (chicken or pork): 4 cups
OR *bouillon cubes:* 3 dissolved in 4 cups water
Chinese dried shrimp: 2 teaspoons
Garlic: 2 cloves, whole
Salt and black pepper: to taste
Vegetable: choice of Bhaji (spinach leaves) OR Jingee (Chinese okra, dishcloth gourd or torchon) OR white pumpkin (white gourd): 2 cups
Corn oil: 1 tablespoon
Egg: 1

Heat oil in pot, add garlic and dried shrimp. When these start to brown, add stock (or bouillon cubes dissolved in water). When liquid starts to boil, add vegetables, and let simmer slowly until cooked. Remove pot from heat and immediately crack the egg and beat up in the boiling soup for a few seconds. The egg will cook in this hot liquid. Add salt and pepper to taste. Serve hot.

Sancoche

Salted pork (pigtail, ribs, etc): 12 oz, cut
   into $1\frac{1}{2}''$ pieces
Stewing beef: 12 oz, cut into $1\frac{1}{2}''$ pieces
Dried split peas: 8 oz
Onions: 2 large, chopped
Celery: 2 stalks, chopped
Thyme: 2 sprigs
Coconut milk (see recipe): 3 cups
Sherry: 4 fluid oz
Ground provisions: $1\frac{1}{2}$ lbs assorted (yam,
   cassava, eddoe, dasheen (taro root),
   peeled and cut into $1\frac{1}{2}''$ pieces
Green 'figs' (unripe bananas): 2, peeled
   and cut into $1\frac{1}{2}''$ pieces
Hot red pepper: 1, left whole
Water or stock: 2 pints
Salt and black pepper: to taste, or
   $\frac{1}{2}$ teaspoon each

Put salted pork and beef in a large pot
with water to cover. Bring to the boil and
cook slowly for 1 hour. Add split peas,
chopped onions, celery, thyme, sherry and
coconut milk and continue to cook at low
to medium heat for 30 minutes.
Add the assorted ground provisions, green
'figs' and corn meal dumplings, and the
hot pepper to lie on top of the ingredients.
Pour the stock to cover and cook for
another 30 minutes.

Corn Meal Dumplings

Yellow corn meal: 3 oz
Flour: 2 oz
Baking powder: 1 teaspoon
Salt: $\frac{1}{4}$ teaspoon
Melted butter: 2 oz

Sift dry ingredients together in a bowl.
Add just enough water, about 3 to 4
tablespoons, to make a light dough. Form
dough into small round balls $\frac{3}{4}''$ in diameter
and roll each in the melted butter.
Put the dumplings into the sancoche pot
for cooking.

Split Pea Soup

Dry green or yellow split peas: 1 package
  (12 or 16 oz)
Salt meat or ham hocks or hambone: 4 oz
  salt meat or 2 ham hocks or 1 ham bone
Hot peppers: 2, whole
Fresh thyme: 2 oz, washed and tied in a
  bunch

Wash peas in a pan or plastic bowl under
slow running water until water is clear and
no longer cloudy. Place a tall pot (always
tall for soups) with 4 pints of water on
stove. Add peas and salt meat or ham.
Cover, bring to boil, turn down heat, and
simmer until peas are broken up. Add
peppers and thyme. Cook until peas
completely dissolved. Add dumplings or
spinners if needed, and cook for further
fifteen minutes. Serve hot.

Garlic Soup

Clear stock – chicken or beef: 4 cups
Garlic: 6 to 8 cloves, crushed
Salt and black pepper: to taste or
  ½ teaspoon each

Put all ingredients into a pot and bring to a
boil, then let simmer for about 20 to 30
minutes. Remove from heat and serve hot,
with or without the garlic in the soup.

Red Snapper and Green Fig Soup

Red Snapper fish: 3 to 4 lbs, cleaned
Fresh lime juice: 2 tablespoons
Ripe tomatoes: 6 medium
Tomato paste: 2 tablespoons
Onions: 2 medium, chopped
Worcester sauce: 2 teaspoons
Water: 3 pints
Salt and black pepper: to taste or 2
  teaspoons
Maraval herbs – chive, thyme, etc:
  1 bunch, wrapped in muslin cloth
Green 'figs': 6, peeled

Bring water to boiling point. Add fresh
herbs, wrapped in muslin cloth, salt, black
pepper and onions. Add fish, tomatoes,
green figs and Worcester sauce. Cook on
low to medium heat for 30 minutes. Remove fish from pot, draining off liquid.
Remove head and bones from fish, add salt
if necessary to suit your taste. Remove the
green figs and tomatoes. Strain the liquid
contents into another pot, using a strainer
or chinois, if you have one. Purée the
green figs, tomatoes and fish (minus head
and bones). Return the purée to soup and
blend. Add lime juice and serve hot.

Ingredients for Red Snapper and Green Fig Soup
Photography by Willie Alleyne. Styling by Marie Henderson

Steam Frying

Over the years, I have enjoyed eating various foods cooked by steaming. The sauce or liquid formed by the steam vapour and meat drippings is subtly blended with the seasonings used. Unlike other methods of cooking where the sauces frequently include additions of stock or veal sauce, the sauces prepared from the liquid drippings of the meat by steaming remain pure. These steam sauces are more subtly implied than assertive, so that the full taste of the meat can be appreciated. Steamed spare ribs in ginger sauce is a good example.

Quick frying also produces a delightful taste to food, imparting the flavour by veneering the seasonings on to the outer surface of the fried food. The limitations of frying, however, demand that only thin slices of meat, poultry or fish can be used, as dehydration and consequent toughening of the food will take place if it is fried for too long a period. The food also runs the risk of burning or carbonising if fried too long.

If both steaming and frying could be combined and integrated into a single process of cooking – STEAM FRYING – by the use of a special cooking vessel to achieve this process, the benefits would be truly rewarding.

We could then cook larger cuts of meat (roast-size), a whole chicken, or a thick steak, without fear of dehydration and toughening of the meat during an extended period of cooking.

1. The meat cooked by steam frying would be browned to a golden colour from frying, while remaining succulent and moist from steaming.

2. It would be a desirable way of cooking for the health and diet conscious, as not much oil would be used.

3. The permeating steam drenching process would tenderise and flavour the meat.

This idea could also be applied for ovens – as steam roasting, steam grilling, and steam broiling.

I felt so strongly that this idea, if implemented, could open a new dimension of cooking. This idea should become a reality with the development of the Steam Fryer, which is expected to become available to the consumer by early 1988. If you are interested, you can write to: 'STEAM FRYER' Box 21292, San Jose, California, 95151–1292, U.S.A.

KAL

Desserts and Cakes

Tropical Fruit—Soursop, Bananas, Oranges and Coconut
Photography by Willie Alleyne. Styling by Marie Henderson

Christmas (Black) Cake

Butter or margarine: 1 lb
Sugar: 1 lb
Eggs: 12
Flour: 1 lb (use a bit more if necessary)
Browning: 4–5 tablespoons (or more)
Vinegar (optional): 1 tablespoon
Flavourings; cinnamon, nutmeg, bitters
    (Angostura): to taste or about 1
    teaspoon
Liquors; Rum: $\frac{1}{2}$ bottle VAT 19
    Stout: 1 pint
    Cherry brandy: 1 pint
    Other liquor if desired
Dried fruits total 4 lbs: 1 lb each raisins
    and prunes, $\frac{1}{2}$ lb currants, citron peel and
    cherries
Almonds and walnuts: $\frac{1}{4}$ lb each if desired

At least 1 month before baking, soak all dried fruit except cherries in the liquor – rum, stout, cherry brandy and/or others with the flavourings – cinnamon powder, nutmeg, bitters, and an additional amount of sugar, about $\frac{1}{2}$ lb. If there is no time for soaking, dried fruits may be boiled with the flavourings and liquors for about $\frac{1}{2}$ hour to make them ready for baking black cake.

Cream butter and sugar and add eggs. Fold in flour, add soaked fruit and cherries, then add browning until desired colour is obtained, and vinegar. Almonds and walnuts can be added if desired. At this point, the mixing spoon should be able to stand up on its own in the cake mixture. One or two handfuls of flour may be added if the mixture is not firm enough. Grease and line cake tins with greaseproof paper, and bake in the oven with the cake tins placed in a pan of water, at 350°F for about 2 hours, until cake is finished – tester comes out clean; or steam in tightly covered tins in water on stove for about $\frac{3}{4}$ hour.

Coconut Ice Cream

Cornstarch or St Vincent arrowroot: 2
    level tablespoons
Gelatin – preferably Davis: 2 pks, or 2
    level tablespoons
Evaporated milk: 2 tins
Condensed milk: 2 tins
Granulated Sugar: $1\frac{1}{2}$ cups or to taste
Coconut water: 5 cups
Coconut jelly: 5 cups medium soft,
    chipped
Coconut milk (see recipe): 2 cups (made by
    grating hard coconut and soaking in
    water, then straining off coconut 'milk')

Boil 2 cups water, dissolve arrowroot in a large pot and add the boiling water slowly to the arrowroot, stirring constantly to avoid making lumps. Add evaporated and condensed milk, dissolve gelatin and add to mixture. If any mixture is lumpy, strain off the lumps. Add sugar, coconut water, finely cut or chipped medium soft coconut jelly, and coconut milk. Taste at this point and add more sugar if a sweeter mix is desired. Freeze, preferably in ice cream freezer. Makes at least 4 quarts.

Dundee Cake

Butter: 1 lb (not so good if margarine is
  used)
Eggs: 10 large or 12 small
Sugar: 1 lb, less 1 tablespoon
Flour: 1 lb, sifted
Baking powder: 2 teaspoons
Dried fruits, total 4 lbs: $\frac{3}{4}$ lb each of
  prunes, citron peel, raisins
  $\frac{1}{2}$ lb each of currants and cherries, red
  and green
Nuts: $\frac{1}{2}$ lb each of walnuts and almonds,
  slit
Vanilla essence: 1 teaspoon
Nutmeg, freshly grated: 1 teaspoon
Bitters: a dash of Angostura

Cream butter and sugar, add eggs, one at a
time. This should be done slowly. Fold in
sifted flour and baking powder, then add
dried fruits and nuts, leaving some cherries
and almonds to decorate top of cake.
Cherries should be both red and green and
cut in half. Add flavourings to taste, but
do not overpower with these. Pour into a
well greased cake tin – for best results use
one with a hole in the centre. Put in oven
at 350°F for $1\frac{1}{2}$ to 2 hours. Test with tester
or tooth pick which should be a slightly
bit sticky, or cake will be overcooked and
a bit dry. Remove from oven and let cool.

Fresh Fruit Delight

Fresh fruit: mango, guava, sapodilla,
  orange, pineapple, pawpaw (papaya) or
  other fresh fruit 1 cup each, sliced
Agar agar (dried Chinese seamoss):
  1 length, about 2″ × 8″
OR *Seamoss,* OR *gelatin:* 2 pks, or
  2 tablespoons
Lemon grass or fever grass: 1 stalk, freshly
  cut
Granulated sugar: 2 tablespoons, or to
  taste
Red cherries: 6
Mint leaves: 1 sprig
Milk: 1 cup

Boil seamoss in about 3 cups water to
which the lemon grass has been added. If
seamoss is not available, boil the lemon
grass, melt the gelatin, and add to the
lemon grass water. Add milk and sugar
and let cool a bit. Slice the fresh fruit and
arrange in serving dishes or large dessert
bowl. Take out lemon grass from the
boiled mixture and discard the grass. Pour
the boiled mixture over the fresh fruit and
let chill for about $\frac{1}{2}$ hour. When the dessert
has set a bit, decorate the top with cherries, mint or other green leaves.

Sponge Cake

Eggs: 3 large
Granulated sugar: 1 cup less about
    1 tablespoon
Flour: 1 cup, sifted at least twice
Baking powder: 1 teaspoon
Hot milk: 1 tablespoon
Grated orange rind: 1 tablespoon – orange
    juice may be used

Beat eggs for 10 minutes, add sugar a little
at a time, then fold in sifted flour. Use the
best quality flour available and sift 4 times
if possible for best results. Add baking
powder, hot milk, then orange (rind or
juice). Pour into a greased cake tin. Best
type is the one with a hole in the middle,
for sponge to come out with best results.
Bake at 350°F for about 25 minutes. Do
not open oven for first 20 minutes as this
can cause cake to fall. Makes 1 cake.

Fish and Crabs

Photography by Willie Alleyne. Styling by Marie Henderson

Miscellaneous Recipes

Clarified Butter

Clarified butter is butter that has been heated and the solids removed when chilled. It is useful for frying or sautéeing as it will stand much greater heat before it begins to burn.

It can be made in several ways.

1. Melt the butter in a saucepan and skim off 'broth' with a perforated spoon.

2. Melt butter under low heat so that it will not burn. Strain it through a fine muslin cloth.

3. Melt butter in a pan with a cupful of water until it becomes frothy. Let it chill until butter becomes solid. Remove the solids. The butter is now clarified.

Caribbean Rum Punch

A popular ditty for this recipe is: ONE, TWO, THREE, FOUR: ONE of sour, TWO of sweet, THREE of strong, FOUR of weak.

Lime juice, (sour): ONE measure from freshly squeezed, peeled limes
Syrup or sugar (sweet): TWO measures
Rum (Trinidad or Barbados) (strong): THREE measures
Water (weak): FOUR measures
Bitters (Angostura): a few shakes from the bottle
Nutmeg (freshly grated): a sprinkle
Red cherries: add when serving

A measure could be in ounces, cups, pints, etc. Mix the liquid ingredients together in a large bowl. Store in clean bottles (labelled and dated). This drink is very popular in the West Indies, and should be treated with respect, or the drinker will know the meaning of 'punch'! It is served very cold – cracked ice is added and the drink is swizzled with a 'chicken foot' swizzle stick. A dash of bitters and a sprinkle of freshly grated nutmeg are added just before serving, and a red cherry if desired. Drink and enjoy.

Cocktail Sauce for Seafood

Tomato ketchup: 1½ cups
Lime juice: 2 teaspoons (2 limes)
Water: ½ cup
Worcester sauce: 3 tablespoons, or to taste
Syrup: 5 teaspoons, or equivalent in sugar
Chive (optional): 2 tablespoons minced
Hot pepper: to taste, or 2 teaspoons of pepper sauce
Salt and black pepper: to taste

Mix all ingredients and add sugar, hot pepper, salt and black pepper to taste. This cocktail sauce can be used with crabmeat, shrimp, lobster, fish, oysters or other seafood.

Hot Pepper Sauce

Hot peppers: 6 large or equivalent in other sizes
Onion: 1 large
Garlic: 1 large or 2 small cloves
Mustard: 1 tablespoon (optional)
Vinegar – white: 1 tablespoon or to taste
Oil – corn or similar: 1 tablespoon
Carrots, cauliflower or other vegetables: ½ cup (optional)
Salt and black pepper: to taste
Sugar: a pinch (optional)
Boiled water: if desired – small amount

Method 1
Mince all ingredients and boil for about 15 minutes. Store in clean, preferably sterilized, glass bottles.
Method 2
Chop finely the hard ingredients and mix with others in a clean container and store in clean, preferably sterilized glass bottles.

Pepper sauce recipes can be adjusted to suit the individual tastes; green paw paw (papaya), green mango, bodi or string beans may also be used instead of, or in addition to the above named vegetables.

Coconut Milk

Coconut milk is an important ingredient in West Indian cooking. It enriches the flavour of the sauces, and is extensively used in meat stews, curries and seafood dishes.

Coconut milk has similar properties and has the same shelf-life as cow's milk. Freshly made coconut milk, when refrigerated, will yield coconut 'cream' which will rise to the top.

Coconut: 2 dried
Boiling water: 1 pint

The dried coconut should contain some coconut water inside. Test by shaking the coconut to see (or hear) if it contains water. Discard if it is totally dry with no water movement inside. In some places, you might not be able to get a dried coconut easily. Check at health-food shops or oriental groceries. A substitute would be dried (dessicated) but unsweetened, coconut flakes. If these are used, substitute cow's milk for water.

Remove the coconut 'meat' from the outer shell by cracking the nut, and prising out the dried coconut 'meat'. The brown outer skin should be removed before the white part is grated. Put contents in a bowl. Pour the boiling water into the bowl and let the grated coconut steep for 15 minutes. If you have a food processor, this can be used instead of grating the coconut. Some cooks do not bother to remove the brown outer skin of the dried coconut before grating.

After the grated coconut has been steeped in the boiling water for 15 minutes or so, strain off the 'milk' with a strainer or fine muslin cloth. Discard the grated coconut after squeezing as much milk out of it as possible. You now have coconut milk ready to use in your recipes. If stored in the refrigerator overnight, coconut cream will form at the surface and can be spooned off.

Mango Chutney

Mangoes: about 6 green, but full – julie, rose, or similar
Vinegar: 1 pint, less a bit
Brown sugar: 1 lb, (or slightly more)
Root ginger: 1 fresh piece, thumb-size
Garlic: 3 cloves, chopped
Raisins: 1 cup
Hot pepper: 1 to 3 or to taste, fresh
Salt: 1 teaspoon or to taste

Peel and slice green mangoes and put to boil (seeds may be added, and taken out later), with vinegar and all other ingredients. When the mixture starts to boil, turn down heat and let simmer until soft, stirring occasionally to prevent burning and sticking. Add a little water only if necessary. Cook for about 1 hour; mixture will darken with cooking. Let cool and bottle in clean, preferably sterile, containers.

Herbs

The mystery of a tasty savoury meal is created by the subtle addition of herbs to the sauce. A sauce should have that special quality of bringing out and enhancing the flavour of the meat itself. It should not be too assertive or overpowering, so as to obscure or dull the taste of the meat or fish. It takes the skill and imagination of a kitchen lover to render and blend herbs subtly into a sauce that would achieve this purpose.

My interest in cooking led me to develop a small hydroponic and undercover garden of herbs and special vegetables. Dill, marjoram, chevril, tarragon, mint, coriander, thyme, celery, parsley and chadon bené (shadow beynay) grow side by side very well. Not only have I made an unsightly area into one of beauty, but it supplies me with all the fresh herbs for my kitchen and friends. Gifts for Christmas to my friends were bottles of herbal vinegar which I had prepared from herbs grown in my garden. I had bought some attractive old apothecary glass bottles in a second hand shop. These were cleaned and sterilized thoroughly and filled with white

Herbal Vinegar

Photography by Willie Alleyne. Styling by Marie Henderson

vinegar. Into each bottle I put assorted herbs, highlighted by brightly coloured small peppers of different shapes and hues. They were sealed and placed in the sun for 4 days during which the flavour of the herbs was assumed into the vinegar. They looked like miniature gardens in each bottle. I tied a little red ribbon at the neck of the bottles.

Herbs originally were used for medicinal cures, and they are still being so used. It was only a matter of time for the beautiful aromas of herbs to find their use into a culinary delight. Most of the herbs in Trinidad are grown in the hills of Maraval by residents of Paramin Village. They are of French Creole descent for several generations. By virtue of its location in the Maraval hills, connected by a very steep, winding road, the Paramin villagers have kept their customs to some extent. French patois is still spoken, and the features of these people are ruddy in complexion and latinesque in appearance. They speak English with the accent of a second language. I can easily recognise them. They grow various herbs in these hills where, apparently, the climatic and soil conditions are ideal for herbs. The chive grown here can be almost as large as a young leek. I believe this particular strain has been propagated for generations. These chives have grown to a remarkably large size which I have not seen anywhere else in my travels to Europe and North America and other places. It is by far more powerful in flavour and aroma than the smaller type of chive, or the scallions, green, or spring onions. For this reason, I suspect it makes West Indian cooking have that special flavour, for chive is used in nearly all the West Indian recipes. The only comparable flavour would be the shallots which are not grown much in Trinidad.

Most countries have their certain preference in their choice of seasonings. Garlic, hot pepper, chive and thyme are the popular seasoning mix in Trinidad. There is another herb called chadon bené (spelt in different ways as shadow beynay, etc) which seems to be peculiar to the West Indies and which is used in cooking meats and stews, as well as fish and other seafood. It grows well in hardy soils, and can thrive without any particular care. It is strongly aromatic and, when cooked in a stew, it completely overpowers and disguises the strong taste of meats like wild meat. It has a flavour somewhat like coriander (Chinese parsley or massala bush), but is more pungent and earthy in flavour. It is excellent for marinating fish that has a high fatty content. One only has to go to Maracas Bay in Trinidad and see the long queue (line) of people buying their fry shark and bake to find out how tasty this can be. Chadon bené is the mystery seasoning.

Herbs like rosemary and tarragon are not much used as seasonings, but more as herbal remedies, in Trinidad. A Paramin villager told me that he would smoke a cigarette with rosemary in it, in order to get rid of a 'head' cold, or he would 'draw' it in boiling water to make a herbal tea, and drink this for medicinal purposes.

Lemon grass, which is excellent for flavouring soups or stocks and grows wild in Trinidad and other West Indian islands is actually used as a tea to get rid of fever, and is popularly known as fever grass. The visitor to the West Indies might find it strange that many herbs are used more for medicinal than for cooking uses.

The *Glossary* in this book will include, not only locally grown herbs, but also the seasonings of other ethnic groups, Trinidad being very multi-racial in character.

Chinese cuisine, which has become internationally popular, is enjoyed in most countries. The essential ingredients used in most Chinese dishes include soy sauce and the derivatives of the soy bean, *dow shee* (black bean), *min-shee* (brown bean), etc and root ginger, chive (scallion or spring onion) and sesame oil. These are some of the basic seasoning ingredients that characterize Chinese cookery. Soy sauce has

now become such an internationally used seasoning agent, that one sees it included in some *nouvelle cuisine* recipes! It would seem that in time, the other soy bean products (black bean, brown bean, etc) as well as other Chinese seasonings, will become more familiar to kitchen lovers, and become a standard part of their seasoning 'armamentarium'.

KAL

Seasonings

Maraval Seasoning

Chive (scallions): 6 fresh stalks
Thyme: 1 small bundle, (fine leaf)
Garlic: 3 cloves, peeled
Onions: 2 medium, peeled
Salt and black pepper: to taste or ½ teaspoon each
White vinegar: to taste or 2 tablespoons
Other herbs: if desired – parsley, etc

Clean chive, cut off hard stalks of the thyme. Purée the seasonings together, then add salt and black pepper and vinegar to taste. Mixture should be a bit liquid; add some boiled water if it is not easy to pour the mixture. Store in a clean, preferably sterilized bottle. Can be kept in refrigerator for at least a month if care is taken to keep it clean and sterile. Do not put spoon – put a dash in storage bottle – pour out small amounts to use at a time, and keep bottle tightly closed when storing.

This seasoning can be added to fish, chicken, pork or beef. It can also be used in salad dressings, sauces, dips, etc.

Smoked Herring Seasoning

Smoked herring: ½ lb smoked herring
Herbs Maraval: 6 bunches – chives (scallions), parsley, thyme, celery, fresh
Garlic: 2 cloves
Red wine vinegar: 2 tablespoons
Sesame oil: 2 teaspoons
Corn oil: 2 tablespoons
Soy sauce: 3 teaspoons (light)
Salt and pepper: to taste
Hot pepper: to taste

Heat and dry the herrings in an oven at 350°F for 30 minutes, or if you have a microwave oven, put in for about 3 minutes. When herring is very dry, grind it into a seasoning salt. Put all the Maraval herbs, garlic, hot pepper and herring salt into a blender and purée contents. Blend in vinegar and oil.

This purée can be stored and used for multifold purposes, and can last for a long time in the refrigerator. This West Indian seasoning can be used for meat or fish or as an additive to stews, sauces and soups, or simply as an hors d'oeuvre filling on pastry. Just add mayonnaise.

The Science of Sauces

A sauce gives a touch of mystery to a meal by its flavouring and consistency. It can be exquisitely delicious, subtle, earthy or overpowering. It can be velvety and smooth in consistency as well as miserably lumpy and pasty. It therefore can be a disaster also. It may take hours, or it can take a couple of minutes to prepare.

Sauces have been developed over the centuries, but it was in the nineteenth century that sauces became more simplified and classified in the French cuisine. Today, it is from these basic sauces, with additions and variations, that many recipes are given added zest and flavour. It is interesting to see how this developed as a result of the French Revolution in that latter part of the eighteenth century.

The French aristocracy had been decimated, and many grand houses were reduced to a point where cooks no longer had unlimited help and some were forced to make a living by their own means, and so restaurants of the finest order came into existence.

Necessity therefore forced the chefs to simplify sauce-making and food preparation to serve meals quickly, as the chefs had to work more on their own and without help as before. It was fortunate that Marie-Antoine Carême (1784 to 1833) was not only a great chef, but also a prolific writer. He was able to classify sauces into 4 families. He used concentrated stock instead of broth, and thickened the sauce with a roux, wheat flour cooked in oil. The four categories of sauces were: the Brown (Espagnole), the Velouté, the Béchamel and the Hollandaise sauces.

These basic sauces with variations and additions developed into a great number of other sauces. This system led to Escoffier's (1902) Guide Culinaire listing 200 different sauces.

The Chinese cuisine, on the other hand, used stocks or broth, and fermented soy bean products for rendering intense flavours to their sauces which were thickened with cornstarch or arrowroot. Cornstarch is a refined pure starch, and is more suitable for thickening a sauce as it gives a more velvety, translucent, lustrous quality to the sauce. Flour, on the other hand, is impure, with at least 10% of solids or proteins. It has to be cooked longer to remove its cereal type (floury) flavour, and if the solids are not removed with a spoon during cooking, it runs the risk of being lumpy, and will render the sauce opaque. Skimming off these extraneous substances was long and tedious, an unnecessary process if cornstarch, a pure starch, were to be used as a thickener.

The Chinese have been using cornstarch for centuries as a thickening agent, and it is ludicrous that cornstarch was regarded as too modern or too recent an ingredient by the French cuisine to be used with classic sauces. One must remember that, in the halcyon days of sauce making before the French revolution, master chefs were coveted and pampered by the aristocracy. In this background, one could quite understand that in this era the cornstarch, which was commonly used for starching clothes, would hardly be considered to be a worthy ingredient for the chefs' prized sauces. To this day, wheat flour is used in a roux for thickening sauces in French recipes. The root starches or tapioca and arrowroot are even better for sauces as they do not have the cereal (floury) flavour. Cornstarch by virtue of its purity, thickens more efficiently than flour, and gives a translucent and glossy appearance to the food it is used in.

Most of the recipes in this book contain starch-based sauces with stock and herbs as the flavourings. Others are gravies made from deglazing the brown solids (as obtained from a roast) with stock, wine or water; or gravies and sauces made from pan-fried juices with the addition of stock. Both are thickened with cornstarch, or arrowroot.

The well-conceived sauce improves the flavour of the food and, visually, the smooth velvet consistency enhances the enjoyment of the dish. But what is the chemistry behind the preparation of this sauce? How does it thicken with just a teaspoon or two of cornstarch dissolved in a little water? It is interesting, if not fascinating to know the science of this process, and I shall attempt to explain it as simply as I can.

Chemistry of Starch-thickened Sauce

Starch chemically consists of thousands of glucose sugar molecules of which there are two kinds. One is called amylose, a linear chain of glucose units, and the other is called amylopectin, a branched structure. Generally, the amylose molecules constitute 20 to 30% of the total.

When cornstarch is mixed with water, it will appear as uniform white opaque liquid, but the granules will eventually settle to the bottom if left to stand for a while. But when the water is heated, or when the cornstarch is put into the stock that is simmering, the character or behaviour of the cornstarch granules changes. The molecules become energised with the heat, and this permits chemical or

hydrogen bonding with the water molecules. In this way, the size of the granules increases until it becomes an enlarged network of starch and water intertwined together. This is the gelatinous or viscous stage. The granules are not so tightly packed as they become diffused, and spread out into a network, and so the opaque suspension becomes clearer and translucent.

With continued heating, the swollen granules break up, and many amylose and amylopectin molecules clone off to link further with other water molecules with hydrogen bonding. With less free water molecules, and less space for them to move freely, the resulting liquid becomes thickened and that is the smooth velvety sauce we refer to in this book.

If you do not understand chemistry, let me explain it in a much simpler way.

Thickening the sauce with cornstarch is like a 'loving experience'. The friendly creatures amylose and amylopectin have many hands and they link up with the equally friendly water molecules until the number of free water molecules is reduced, and they slow down because there is not much space for them to move about freely, and so everything slows down to result in the 'friendly' thickened or 'cosy' sauce!

KAL

Sorrel: Drink and 'Fruit'   Photography by Willie Alleyne. Styling by Marie Henderson